Notes from a Native Son

Notes from a Native Son

Essays on the Appalachian Experience

Garry Barker

The University of Tennessee Press • Knoxville

First Edition.

The paper in this book meets the minimum requirements of the American National Standard for Permanence of Paper for Printed Library Materials.
∞
The binding materials have been chosen for strength and durability.

Library of Congress Cataloging-in-Publication Data

Barker, Garry, 1943—
Notes from a native son: essays on the Appalachian experience / Garry Barker.—1st ed.
p. cm.
Includes bibliographical references and index
ISBN 0-87049-900-9 (pbk.: alk. paper)
1. Appalachian Region, Southern—Social life and customs. 2. Kentucky—Social life and customs. 3. Handicraft—Appalachian Region, Southern. 4. Handicraft—Kentucky. I. Title.
F217.A65B37 1995
974—dc20 95-4356
CIP

To Wanda Vice and Emily Ann Smith,
the two teachers who "let" me write
as much as I wanted,
about whatever I wanted,
but insisted always that I write it well.

Contents

Foreword *Jim Wayne Miller* ix
Preface xi

Part 1. ***Learning***
Notes from a Native Son 3
Your Turn: The *Courier-Journal* Essays 10
A Generation of "In-betweeners" 31
Slings and Arrows 40
Appalachian Voices 55
Stranger than Truth 86

Part 2. ***Working***
I Still Love to Mow 95
Working 96
Writing about the Crafts 111
Romancing the Crafts 116

Part 3. ***Laughing***
Humor Is as Humor Does 125
Head of the Holler 130

Part 4. ***Looking***
Many Hands Make Light Work 189

Notes 199
Bibliography 203

Foreword

Garry Barker's *Notes from a Native Son* includes essays and opinion pieces written, for the most part, during the 1980s and early 1990s. But these writings reflect not only the events and issues of the decade in which they were written, they also draw on the author's experience of growing up in Appalachian Kentucky in the 1940s and 1950s, a time of wrenching change, and upon his historical awareness of his region and its relation to the rest of the country. While they are essays based on Barker's particular Appalachian experience, they offer valuable insights and perspectives for anyone interested in the general experience of the Appalachian region's people and in the region's past, present, and future.

These *Notes from a Native Son* are genuine essays; that is, attempts to clarify, to understand, to connect the past with the present, to glimpse the future, to determine what was good and what might still be, to characterize the conflicts, discontinuities, the pain and pleasure of living in a particular time and place. To read these essays is to witness a thoughtful and fair-minded man in the act of working through, first for himself, then for us, issues central to the collective life of southern Appalachia; to read them is to witness a man thinking hard, trying to make sense out of his own experience and the experiences of the region's people.

Part 1, "Learning," effectively blends direct personal experience with thoughtful responses to issues, agencies, and individuals, and to books and films that have been influential in the region. Vivid word pictures alternate with reflections on the Council of the Southern Mountains, federal arts subsidies, Harriette Arnow's *The Dollmaker* as book and film, a poignant trip home to Elliott County for a funeral, and personal observations on the writing of fiction. Part 2, "Working," offers both a personal experience of administration in the crafts world as well as a historical perspective of the crafts industry in Appalachia. Here, as in part 1, we find the same evenhandedness in assessing people, institutions, and issues. Part 3, "Laughing," is made up of humorous pieces on subjects ranging from grits to grandchildren, from regional speech and stereotypes to snakes and shot-up road signs.

Toward the end of *Notes* Barker identifies himself as "half hillbilly, half yuppie, half redneck activist" and then, realizing "that's too many halves," adds a couple more! This is but one of several ways in which he demonstrates the inadequacy of stereotypes, off-the-rack opinions, and other varieties of conventional wisdom, with respect to both individuals or to the southern Appalachian region with which he is concerned.

What emerges from these essays is a portrait of their author, whose complexity is to a great degree a reflection of his region and its history. While he constantly probes, compares, and questions, he does not always provide answers, for he would rather ask the right question than offer a specious answer. Yet *Notes* does suggest its own worth and usefulness. Commenting at one point on the pleasure he derived as a young man from mowing branchbanks and hayfields, Barker observes, "I still love to mow. You can see where you've been." Reading his essays, we can better see where both he and his region have been during the past half century.

Jim Wayne Miller

Preface

Most of the books and articles about us are written by someone else—someone from somewhere else, someone who came, saw, studied, compared, and wrote about this sometimes bizarre little piece of America called "Appalachia." Seldom has the native voice spoken with the credibility assigned to the outsider, the missionary, the sociologist, the folklorist, the sensationalist, the learned expert who frequently entirely misses the subtle humor, quiet pain, intense pride, and bridled passion that are part of every native mountaineer.

There are a handful of major exceptions: Cratis Williams, Harry Caudill, Loyal Jones, and Jim Wayne Miller, to name just a few, speak from an inside viewpoint, a perspective that acknowledges an imperfect reality but expresses a love for the culture that cannot be so easily defined and classified as many would have you believe.

For more than twenty years now, my biased, sometimes jaundiced, sometimes sentimental voice has cropped up here and there in the region's journals and newspapers, and much of the material herein originally appeared in the *Louisville Courier-Journal,* the *Lexington Herald-Leader, Appalachian Heritage,* and other publications with more than a passing concern for issues Appalachian.

Maybe the answer was best explained by my then teen-aged daughter when I told her she'd catch less grief if sometimes she'd simply keep her mouth shut. "I know, Dad," she said with a grin. "But sometimes if I didn't speak up I'd just bust."

Sometimes, if I didn't write out my frustrations, I'd just bust.

I definitely am not a folklorist, historian, or sociologist. I am not a trained anything, by academic standards; I just blunder along on instinct and emotion, crossbred with the bleak reality and scarred outlook of a native son who has endured and survived and who is compelled to write about it.

My family is from Elliott County, Kentucky, from ten generations of hardy, hard-working, hard-playing, hard-headed mountaineers. I'm the third oldest of nine kids, a "war baby," part of the now middle-aged generation that has *lived* the changes that jerked the mountains a hundred years forward in just a few tumultuous decades.

I'm more hillbilly than Appalachian, more redneck than quaint mountaineer.

Should you read on, you'll hear all of that. And you'll see, quickly, that I don't live in either a rose-colored world of romantic illusion or in a bleak, hopeless fog of helplessness.

But there's some of both. My world is neither perfect nor pathetic. How I view it depends largely on how I feel today. How I wrote what I wrote, then, depended on how I felt at the time. The emphasis on crafts comes, simply, from the work I've done since 1965. That's what I do: that's part of what I write about.

But I was born here, have lived here for fifty years, don't ever plan to live anywhere else.

That's just the way it is.

Part 1

Learning

Notes from a Native Son

At a thirty-year high school reunion, a classmate and I—we hadn't seen each other since graduation night in 1961—surprised ourselves by remembering so much.

She had envied, she said, my schoolboy focus and accomplishment, my grades, my mathematical ability and sure sense of direction.

I chuckled, recalled how insecure and terrified I'd been most of the time, then told her how much I'd admired her poise, maturity, creativity, and social ease, her independent actions and thinking. "I just did what they told me, believed everything they said," I remembered. "But you, you made your own decisions."

We shared a wistful laugh at how intimidated each had been by the other, how envious, how naive.

I started high school in 1957 with mud on my shoes, empty pockets, a mountain accent, and a robotic notion that I would learn all the great things the faculty and books had to offer.

Being a farm kid from a rural elementary school, I was automatically assigned to classes in vocational agriculture and general math. I already knew more than I ever wanted to know about farming, and by the fifth grade I'd gone well beyond anything that basic math class would cover.

I used up my small stock of nerve getting myself freed from the ag course. I didn't even bother to buy a book for general math. But the next year I plowed happily into algebra and advanced English and—except for the social barriers—had high school under control.

So I stepped the effort up a notch, worked so hard to break out from my shy, tongue-tied, inferiority-ridden personality that I earned (and treasured) the tag of "smartass." By my senior year I was student body president, prom king, one of Kentucky's early National Merit Scholarship semifinalists, and—much to my surprise—a Thespian.

On stage, in someone else's personality, life was easy: looking back after thirty-five years, it's easier to see how all the acting I did every day in the halls and classrooms was so neatly transferred to formal dramatics.

At home, perhaps unintentionally, I was getting a mixed message: plenty of encouragement and support, but always tempered with a caution not to expect too much. Lower expectations meant less failure and disappointment; my mother was afraid my accomplishments, my breaking across established social barriers, and my naive enthusiasm would hurt too much when the bubble burst.

Her freely given words of comfort were "God must have loved poor people, He made so many of us." Some days those words helped numb a nameless pain, but on good days they simply fueled the stubborn determination to make some changes.

To offset being poor, being a "hillbilly," being one of nine kids, I created an alter ego, a wise-cracking, laid-back public personality, which worked. I deliberately missed test questions so I wouldn't have the highest score; learned to poke fun at my poverty-level, hayseed existence; ignored the blatant racism that was part of everyday life; dated the mayor's daughter (and vastly underestimated *her* ability to understand and appreciate what I really was, not what I pretended to be); and sort of had the high school world at my fingertips.

But high school only lasts four years.

And, I suddenly realized, graduation would slap me squarely back into the ranks of low-paid labor, back where maybe I really belonged.

But there were scholarship offers and determined faculty members pushing hard to see that I went to college. I traveled to Lexington for interviews at the University of Kentucky and Transylvania College and came home terrified; the social sophistication, money, new cars, and big-city settings brought out my worst fear: that my backwoods reality would be publicly exposed and ridiculed at either place.

So I packed up what little I owned and came to Berea, where they said simply that they'd find a way, financially, to get me through.

I'd never, at the time, even heard of Berea College. But, according to the printed materials and the people I discovered in Fleming County who'd gone there, Berea was the school for Appalachians, the poor, the mountain kids with the ability but not the money for college. I went to Berea believing that I'd finally found a place where I could just be me.

It *almost* was. Nobody in Berea knew or cared very much who I was or where I was from. But Berea also gave me a very mixed message regarding my heritage; in 1961 there were no classes in Appalachian literature or history, no Appalachian center and museum, no special effort to recognize and appreciate the mountain culture.

Adapt, I was told. Adjust. Learn to speak English. Cast off your hillbilly beliefs, practices, religion, and personality. But look the other way, while we use your history, your poverty, and your heritage to raise the money we need to finance making you over into a proper middle-class midwesterner.

It was good professional and social advice, excellent preparation for life after college, but—I felt then—a hypocritical denial of what had first drawn me to Berea.

I went from the top of the class to the bottom, from perfect nerd to fringe radical, and worked just enough to get by and get a degree. My test scores were so high that Berea was reluctant to give up on me, and in the English department I found enough encouragement and pressure to get me through. I also found Emily Ann Smith, then the department chair, who didn't teach Appalachian authors in her classes but first pointed me to the work of Harriette Arnow. And for the next twenty years, Miss Smith was to greet me always with her brilliant smile and the same question. "When," she'd ask, "are you going to write?"

I shocked the faculty (and myself) at graduation by accepting a low-paying job as a sort of do-gooder, a nonprofit administrator, and the challenge of doing real work after four years of playacting was strong enough to bring out the best in me.

Bob Gray, then director of the Southern Highland Handicraft Guild, stressed organization, preparation, decisive action, and learning. Every project, every event, every trip was an opportunity.

The Grays—Bob and Verdelle—are to this day two of my closest friends. But even my mentor and I could disagree: Bob Gray loves the Appalachian humor, skill, and sense of survival, and his image of the independent, stoic mountaineer is embodied in Pa Walton of the TV series. Mr. Gray never seemed to relate to my sarcastic references to the Walton family's land, huge bathroom-equipped house, cars, sawmill, and prominent position in the community.

In *The Waltons* there was no harsh poverty or hopelessness, none of the endless frustration that often leads to drinking and shooting, no hillbilly jokes, none of the bawdy, almost rowdy humor I know and love.

Idyllic Walton's Mountain may very well have existed. But I never saw it, or anything close to it.

And, instead of judging poor people who needed help, I fumed at the inadequate efforts that were part of the "War on Poverty" being fought all around me during the turbulent mid-1960s.

I come from a line of poor, proud, self-sufficient people whose lives were disrupted when a cash economy came to northeast Kentucky. After more than two centuries of living off the land, almost overnight—in the larger scheme of time—we were dependent upon electricity, mail-order catalogs, prepackaged foods, ready-made clothes, cars, and the other things we needed or wanted but that had to be purchased.

Many of my aunts and uncles simply moved away, after World War II, to places where jobs and easier living outweighed the ties to home and culture.

Harriette Arnow's *The Dollmaker* is modern Appalachia's classic novel, the first book to capture the disruption of a culture. It's bleak, barren, difficult, depressing reading. But *The Dollmaker* reflects reality, in a way no other mountain novel really does, and—paired with Arnow's *Hunter's Horn*—can serve as the required reading for all those who would understand this region.

Harriette Arnow is the reason I continue to write, to struggle to put into words the world that shapes an Appalachian native, to try and offset the contradictory images of the mountaineer as either noble white savage or welfare-dependent, inbred animal who fouls his own nest.

Both extreme images stem from truth, from reports to the "outside" world by sometimes well-meaning but sensation-seeking reporters of this highly studied, largely misunderstood region.

We all have our own perceptions of our own worlds, but Appalachia has been dissected so often—and so often by sociologists, folklorists, and scholars from somewhere else—that native voices are usually ignored.

We who are from the region far too often sell out, say what we think people want to hear, try to imitate the academic studies we read and discuss.

Researchers usually prefer dried, yellowed books over real, imperfect people; so much of what is written today simply perpetuates past written stereotypes.

When David Whisnant dug through the records and published *All That Is Native and Fine,* his indictment of the cultural manipulation of Appalachia by some of our foremost individuals and institutions, he earned instant hatred from much of the world that still effectively manages that subculture. Whisnant said "bad things about good people," about music, crafts, and educational philosophies imposed on a people by essentially well-meaning missionaries during the early part of this century.

I agree with a lot of Whisnant's conclusions. The major difference in our viewpoints, I suspect, is that while he studied the culture, I lived it. And I know, firsthand, about the love-hate relationship we have—and have had for a hundred years—with those who would stoop to help us.

We are grateful for the humane effort, we love many of the good people who've given their lives to this region, but there's an undercurrent of resentment. We needed the help but would have preferred to receive it without so many strings attached, without the stern disapproval of the way we live, without the effort to make us over.

Even John Day's valuable book *Bloody Ground,* which I recommend almost daily as the best description of what life once was in eastern Kentucky, was written from a disapproving viewpoint. Day's superb journalism and descriptions outweigh his judgments, but he, like most, neither understood nor liked the native mountaineer.

Of current writers, southwest Virginia native Lee Smith best captures, without judgment, the strengths and weaknesses of Appalachia. Sassy, irreverent, and real, Smith's characters are imperfect, impulsive, human, and alive, vividly accurate descriptions of past and present personalities. She paints neither totally heroic figures nor hopeless despair; Lee Smith's fiction is *real.* Her characters, like most living, breathing people, can be as weak and wrong as they can be strong and right.

In my own fiction I tend to lean toward the rascal, the maverick, the sort-of-renegade who has been judged deficient by normal measurements but who proves those presumptions to be wrong.

Yes, I *am* a lifelong O. Henry fan. But that's just part of it.

Perhaps because I've spent so much of my fifty years pretending to be something I'm not, I lean toward characters who are much more than they appear to be, characters who are initially judged by outward appearance and stereotype but who ultimately reveal a depth and quality no one had suspected.

Probably because of my own life and career ups and downs, the fringe characters appeal to me.

I don't know. As Jim Wayne Miller says in the introduction to these essays, I offer questions far more often than I offer answers.

If I *knew* the answers to all my questions, I probably wouldn't still be writing, sifting, and sorting, working toward some acceptable personal understanding of just who I am. Nearly a half century of adapting and adjusting, of rediscovery and revision, of reading and writing, of loving and fighting, has surely created a more complex personality than can be explained away in a handy stereotype.

I think my own life, and the lives of thousands of other native Appalachians, has been made more complicated by the expectations—good and bad—assigned to us by the studied experts. It's hard to be quaint, noble, and pure at the same time you're cooking down some moonshine, fighting a feud, or reading the condescending and inaccurate words of Jack Weller's *Yesterday's People.*

It's hard to be isolated from the world when you have a 120-channel satellite TV hookup, when you've been Uncle Sam's cannon fodder for 200 years, when you're part of one of the most written about, studied, and misunderstood cultures in the world.

This collection of thought, outrage, reporting, and humor is, as implied, just one native son's changing view of his changing world. The essays and columns express what I felt when I felt it. I changed, over the years, just as did our culture and our way of life. The crafts emphasis reflects the world I knew best.

I have never attempted to impose my opinions upon anyone else, but I've fought stubbornly for my right to those opinions.

I don't know where I'm going, but I do know where I've been.

Your Turn

The *Courier-Journal* Essays

For many decades the Bingham family's *Louisville Courier-Journal* was the newspaper for issues about Kentucky and or Appalachia, the daily reading for anyone concerned with excellence and depth in reporting and writing.

It was for the *Courier-Journal* op-ed series, "Your Turn," that I first hesitantly wrote my opinionated observations, and most of those early works dealt with the crafts world that had been my life—then—for over fifteen years.

My first "Your Turn" contribution was a response to Ronald Reagan's proposed cuts to funding for the National Endowment for the Arts budget. Perhaps still stinging from my controversial departure after ten years as executive director of the Kentucky Guild of Artists and Craftsmen, and feeling a little cheapened by years of pretending to understand and appreciate art that has to be footnoted, I wrote, in 1981, "Has the Federal Money Given to the Arts Done More Harm than Good?"

President Reagan's suggested cut of 50 percent in the funding for the National Endowment for the Arts has provoked a passionate protest in the arts world. A close look at the complainers will provide some insight into the reasons a drastic budget reduction (or total elimination) is in order.

The National Endowment for the Arts (NEA) has funded some excellent projects in keeping with the congressional mandate of delivering art to the people, but it's also financed an elitist, self-serving series of inside projects that ensures that the same small group reaps most of the benefit.

NEA estimates that only 2 percent of Americans are involved

in the arts as patrons or participants; the other 98 percent share in the financing but not in the proceeds. Very likely only 2 percent of the nation's artists have benefited from the endowment funds, and the other 98 percent are resentful and critical of the funding process.

I've dealt with the endowment—primarily the visual arts programs—since the beginning in 1965. Frankly, I think the money has done more harm than good.

Panels of handpicked "experts" award grants to their friends, and individual grants go largely to a "Who's Who" of East or West Coast artists and craftsmen.

The NEA staff subtly maneuvers organizations through control of eligibility guidelines, then pressures artists for support when a larger funding package is being pushed through Congress.

Government intervention in anything assures mediocre results. The arts, freest and most spontaneous of all forms of expression, are restricted by guidelines and dulled by an evaluation system that starts with egotistic experts and ends with bureaucratic numbers and red tape.

Grants create an unhealthy dependency. Individuals and organizations compete for expansion money, use it to start all-new projects, and then are left hanging in uncertain limbo when funds are pulled.

"Matching funds," the subtle misnomer used to apply most funding, forces deceit or entrapment. Shrewd grant recipients quickly learn to pad the figures and stretch the truth; the more naive learn—often too late—that there's no such thing as a free lunch.

Government is a provider of services—mail, defense, welfare—those items supposedly delivered more efficiently on a large scale.

Art does not adapt to the mass-delivery concept.

Art is too personal, impossible to disseminate and measure from Washington.

NEA funds all fifty state arts councils. How many legislatures would continue the local appropriations if the federal funds weren't there? Would Kentucky cough up the cash to continue?

Art organization functions best at the local levels that are least funded. Local groups, the only ones able to respond quickly to local needs, are generally left to their own means. Efficiency decreases and funding increases at higher levels, and Washington decisions are made in a vacuum.

The president should proceed with little fear of public outrage. Few of the vocal 2 percent voted for him anyway, and the other 98 percent couldn't care less. He'll lose a few votes by cutting the budget of the National Endowment for the Arts; he'll gain mine by totally eliminating federal intervention in the arts.

The final reports required from endowment grantees are complicated and ambiguous, but that doesn't matter since they're not read anyway.

Federal money spawned a core of so-called "arts administrators," some trained in special programs at Harvard and others by NEA internships. These are the grant writers and fund raisers, the professional users of public money.

Nobody knows for sure just how many exist; I'd hazard a guess of ten thousand, almost all paid by federal funds in one way or the other. These would be the major casualties of a budget cut; few practicing artists would ever feel the difference.

The arts survived before there was a National Endowment, and they will survive again without a federal patron. Before NEA, the arts profession was more selective, more competitive, but the good, dedicated artists made it.

Obviously, before 1965, arts patrons found a way to fund their own programs, free from federal guidelines and panels of experts, and the system worked. A "free market" of the arts gave each person the choice of whether a program or a person was worthy of support.

The endowment, funded by all the people, imperiously decided for us which artists were worthy.

You won't find NEA money in the movie theaters or at rock-music concerts; federally decreed good taste does not include tole (lacquered or enameled metalware) painting or hillbilly music. Who decides what is good or bad? The experts. The selected panels. The 2 percent. The rest of us just pay the bills.[1]

> The response was, looking back after all the years, predictable. All hell broke loose in federally funded Kentucky art circles.

Moritz Bomhard, then artistic director of the Kentucky Opera Association, wrote for the *Courier-Journal* that my "naivete" was "so obvious that anyone who is seriously concerned with the arts will dismiss it. . . ." He argued that without continuing federal arts support the people who live in Louisville "would lose just about everything that makes living in this town bearable—a live orchestra, a ballet company, a superb and now well renowned theater, an opera company. . . ."

He added that "Of course, there aren't many people who care whether John Doe weaves a basket somewhere in the hinterlands or paints some primitive picture" and defended NEA procedures by saying "The people who make up our government are not only too busy, but they are illiterate when it comes to artistic matters, and they are fair enough to know that artistic decisions ought to be made by artists."

"History shows," Mr. Bomhard ended his article, "that it never was a majority of the people who participated in the arts, but it also shows us that it is the artistic climate of a certain time and place which made possible the growth of truly civilized human beings. Mr. Barker can apparently do without them."[2]

My response from the "hinterlands" was that, yes, I could do without the artistic elitists, and that if there's nothing else Mr. Bomhard likes about Kentucky then he should leave.

This initial experience with the press stung, to say the least, but it strengthened my stubborn resolve, and I still agree with my initial, instinctive response to Mr. Bomhard.

I then began to even more firmly believe it was time to stop looking the other way, time to stop accepting concepts I could not—deep down—really endorse, time to add one more voice to the editorial debates.

I wanted to develop the voice of a "native son," the sort of rawboned redneck who'd learned to read and write, the ordinary Kentuckian who'd kept his mouth shut for far too long.

> But such grand ideas must be approached gradually. My next "Your Turn" in the *Courier-Journal* was a plea to Phyllis George Brown, our new first lady, to at least acknowledge all the work that went into making sure Kentucky's crafts were here, strong, and developed, just waiting to be discovered.

Phyllis George Brown's "discovery" of Kentucky crafts is a welcome shot in the arm for the industry, a perfect example of how one sparkling personality can create a happening.

The attendant publicity helps every Kentucky craftsman; the stimulus of buyers from Bloomingdales' and Marshall Field's has caught the attention of every craft producer in the state, and the glamour of helicopters, New York names, and Miss America has proven irresistible.

Will it last?

Hold that question. Go back to the beginning. Kentucky craftsmen have been here from the beginning, since the state was settled, and many still work in the same place as their forebears. Isolation kept the crafts alive for over a century, and then a dedicated group of individuals and organizations took over.

Berea College led the way. In 1904, according to newspaper accounts, the college's commencement day was a regional craft fair, a busy showing of quilts and coverlets, handwoven baskets, and hickory-bottomed chairs. Later, the college and the Council of the Southern Mountains (then the Conference of Southern Mountain Workers) helped organize the Southern Highland Handicraft Guild in 1929. Berea was headquarters to the organization during its early years and continues to provide much of the leadership to the venerable and thriving agency.

At Bybee, the Cornelisons have operated Bybee Pottery for at least 160 years, in the same building. Mr. and Mrs. D. C. Churchill opened Churchill Weavers in 1921, and their handbuilt looms are still in use. The settlement schools—in Pine Mountain, Hindman, Annville, and Red Bird—kept the crafts as part of their community program, and the Berea College Student Craft Industries grew into perhaps the world's largest production-training center for the crafts.

The Kentucky craft movement was clarified in 1960 by a combined effort. Gov. Bert T. Combs created the Arts and Crafts Division of the Kentucky Department of Commerce, and a group of "craft evangelists" formed the Kentucky Guild of Artists and Craftsmen. For almost eight years the state worked in marketing, in projects ranging from a Kentucky catalog to massive training programs, and the guild crossed the state with the Kentucky Guild Train, a Berea-based pair of Southern Railway boxcars that carried exhibits and workshops to every Kentucky city served by the rails.

At the same time, in the late 1960s, the federal War on Poverty was helping create craft-production cooperatives across eastern Kentucky.

Perhaps the turning point came in 1967, the year of the first Kentucky Guild Fair. That event paved the way for hundreds of similar events, and over the years a half-million people have come to Indian Fort Theater at Berea for the fairs.

The guild's volunteer leadership came from a broad circle. Names such as Virginia Minish, Clara Eagle, Lester Pross, Rude Osolnik, Jane Samples, Ernie Cornelison, and Smith Ross should be engraved on the invoices of every current producing craftsman. Those people built today's thriving market, turned a vision into reality, and did it out of a love for the crafts.

Kentucky crafts are not new to New York City. A shop in the Rockefeller Center operated for years; a 1968 feature at Georg Jensen, a fine-crafts outlet, spotlighted Kentucky and Appalachia.

Also, Kentucky has been featured in the Smithsonian's Festival of American Folklife; Kentucky is represented in every major craft show, events such as the five-million-dollar Baltimore Winter Market, and Kentuckians serve on the selection panels for many of the national shows.

Fifteen years ago the only craft shop of consequence in Kentucky was the Log House Sales Room in Berea. Today, in Berea alone there are a dozen shops; Louisville and Lexington offer excellent showings, and MATCH, Inc., has even crossed over the river to open The Appalachia Shop in Cincinnati.

State support began with Governor Combs and continued; Govs. Wendell Ford and Julian Carroll provided continuing, stabilizing funds to strengthen the crafts. The state parks have made fumbling efforts to incorporate the crafts, hindered always by red tape and a reluctance to make a quality judgment. The state arts commission has given strong support, especially in the areas of administration and education.

Will it last?

Yes. The Kentucky craft movement—the industry—is firmly established, a tradition and rapidly growing economic factor, a force that organized itself over the years and moves forward on the basis of heritage and quality.

Mrs. Brown has neatly utilized the crafts as a promotional vehicle and has brought a new wave of interest to the profession (plus an equally healthy surge of orders). But if past experience is any indication of the future, the big, trendy stores will stay with the crafts until the newsworthiness ends, then quietly slip back to their usual lines of factory-produced goods.

The craftsmen will shrug it off, go back to their established markets, and be richer for the experience.

My conclusion?

Thanks, Mrs. Brown, for an injection of personality and publicity. But please, sometime, somewhere along the line stop and pay tribute to the people who did the hard work.[3]

> A few short years later I was defending the same Mrs. Brown, showing how my views had changed, in the following "Your Turn" effort.

All three of the major Democratic gubernatorial candidates, in response to a Department of the Arts query, expressed support for continuing the state-level effort to market handcrafts.

That's good, but no one could really expect a candidate to knowingly alienate a large and growing block of potential voters.

And no one can replace Phyllis George Brown as an attention-getting spokesperson for the handcraft industry. For four years, Mrs. Brown has forcefully promoted Kentucky's crafts in ways previously impossible; the solid, two-hundred-year-old craft culture has benefited tremendously from the glamour and vitality she injected.

There are, of course, those in Kentucky's arts community who sniff and disapprove, look down their noses, and call Mrs. Brown a tacky opportunist, who insist she has used the crafts to further her own image and gain personal publicity.

Who cares?

Even if the offended artists were correct—and they're not—Mrs. Brown's efforts have helped Kentucky's craftspeople gain the attention they have always deserved but have never received.

Kentucky's handcraft industry has been here since the beginning: what was perhaps the nation's first craft fair was held in Berea in 1896, a "Homespun Fair" that celebrated Berea College's commencement day. Many individuals, organizations, and previous governors contributed to the tremendous growth of the industry from 1960 to 1980, and Kentucky has long been recognized in professional circles as a leader in quality handcraft production.

Mrs. Brown extended Kentucky's reputation to a national audience, through national magazines and network television, through sheer personality and persistent effort.

I was a skeptic, at first, and I still disagree with part of the image Mrs. Brown has projected for Kentucky crafts. But I'm a firm believer, now, in the power of personality and the sincerity of the effort. Phyllis George Brown has opened new doors and created exciting possibilities, and she will hand the next administration a rare opportunity to keep those doors open and develop solid service systems for the crafts.

The new governor cannot possibly match Phyllis George Brown's show-business flair and personal contacts, but he or she can continue the official state recognition of handcrafts as a profession and an industry.

We've learned—the hard way—that the state itself has no business trying to directly market crafts (except through existing systems such as the state parks). Gov. Bert T. Combs's Arts and Crafts Division, once part of the Department of Commerce, opened a craft warehouse and a string of retail stores that failed; Louis Nunn switched the arts and crafts to the Department of Parks and built in a top-heavy administrative structure of political appointees.

Combs's effort cannot be called a total failure. The work of the Arts and Crafts Division helped build the Kentucky Guild of

Artists and Craftsmen, drew national attention and funding, and set in motion an effort that has continued, in some form, for over twenty years. John Y. Brown, in the reorganized Department of the Arts, elevated the crafts back to separate divisional status, and Crafts Coordinator Karen Horseman has done a superb job there.

It is to be hoped that the new governor will retain the current structure and the emphasis on crafts.

The role of Kentucky crafts in the state's advertising can be expanded; the work being done in West Virginia and North Carolina is a good example. Crafts are a major drawing card for tourism—Kentucky's strongest growth industry—and deserve a more prominent role in the state promotion.

The new governor, by decree, could resolve a twenty-year-old debate about selling Kentucky crafts in the state park gift shops.

The Department of Parks has proven, consistently, that it cannot and/or will not implement a quality craft marketing program. The solution is simple. Give the authority to someone else, either by management contract or by departmental restructuring, and make a committed, qualified effort. Use the Kentucky Arts Council and the Crafts Division as advisors and maintain current budgets for purchasing and personnel. There comes a time, after twenty years of frustration, when the only solution is to bypass the problem area.

A continuing business-education program is needed. Craftspeople are, basically, small-business people; their education normally has not prepared them for the daily problems of production, marketing, and record-keeping.

The new administration will not have the dynamic Phyllis George personality to draw attention and create openings, but it can record some solid accomplishments by taking full advantage of what has already been done.

And—depending on how she was asked—Mrs. Brown might continue to make use of her extensive contacts to promote Kentucky. This would require some setting aside of politics and ego, but the results might be worth the effort.[4]

In the spring of 1982, I wrote the first of my "Appalachian" essays for the *Courier-Journal,* my first stubborn and emotional statement from the "native" viewpoint, and it ran as "Upgrading the Image of Appalachia."

Last month, at Annville Institute in Jackson County, I was part of a regional conference with the theme of "Appalachian Heritage," a positive gathering of dedicated workers who deal daily with the housing, economic development, and social welfare of the region.

Two films were shown at the sessions sponsored by a committee of the Commission on Religion in Appalachia. The first described Appalachians as "drenched in filth and ignorance." The second almost movingly described shacks where children walked barefoot through human excrement on the floors and in the yard.

The films—admittedly 1960s productions—were supposedly pro-Appalachian. Afterwards, not even the compassionate descriptions of displaced Appalachians offered by Ernie Mynatt, who works with them in Cincinnati for the Appalachian Fund, could soothe my ruffled feathers. I'm tired of being told—by "friendly" forces—that I'm inferior.

I grew up in that "substandard" housing so often discussed—no running water or indoor bathrooms, no central heat, eleven of us in about six hundred square feet—but I was never drenched in anything but love, stubborn pride, and a determination to get an education so I wouldn't have to be poor anymore.

Blanket indictments of Appalachia are no more valid than condemnations of any other people or region. We don't all live in coal camps. Some parts of eastern Kentucky didn't have any industry; maybe we were the more fortunate ones.

My ancestors are Irish and Scotch, tough and industrious workers who've lived in Elliott County for eight or ten generations, scraping a living from tobacco, timber, trapping, or whatever came along. Most of us left the county after World War II—my parents took us to the eastern edge of Fleming County, a place where good schools were available. All nine of us eventually graduated from Fleming County High School—with no public assistance of any kind—and with test scores above the national average.

Even in Fleming County—now defined as part of Appalachia—we were considered the hillbillies, people who talked funny and practiced a strange culture. I quit talking and started writing when they laughed at my Appalachian pronunciation; even Berea College tried—without notable success—to alter my speech patterns. I was just out of college and working in the North Carolina mountains when the War on Poverty broke loose in Appalachia. I watched the movies being made, read the books and magazine articles about us, saw millions of dollars wasted, and fumed at the image presented to the nation.

Innovative writers, producers, and professional antipoverty workers fed the nation a story that was true—to a degree—but that confirmed our image of ignorance and futility. The very people who rage and froth at the mouth about the way *Hee Haw* and *The Beverly Hillbillies* degrade Appalachia did much more serious and permanent damage by officially perpetuating the concept of cultural deficiency. To raise more money, the professionals effectively stamped us as inbred, filthy, shiftless, and moronic.

Some of us are.

But, then, so are some of you.

World War II, television, mobile homes, consolidated schools, and decent highways have forever altered the mountains. Now our children eat the same national-brand junk foods, watch the identical mediocre television, are fed the same bland educations, and want the same things as do kids anywhere else. We now have marijuana, VD, acid rock, divorce, and alcoholism, just like the rest of the country.

Dukes of Hazzard is probably Appalachia's number one TV series. Bad? Not necessarily. The show is no more inane than *Dallas,* no more unreal than *Diff'rent Strokes.* On the *Dukes* show, the good guys always win; the hillbillies always outfox the city slickers. That part, sadly, is wishful thinking. For about two hundred years, the city slickers have been winning, bleeding Appalachia, leaving us with deserted coal camps and destroyed mountainsides, succeeding in making the world believe it was all our fault.

Many of us Appalachians live in an eerie time warp, with one foot forever lodged in the recent past. I rode a mule-powered wagon down Sinking Creek to Olive Hill to get my first haircut, shoes, and tinted photograph; twenty-five years later I was hopping jets for cross-country travel, living in a golf-course subdivision, and drinking cocktails with senators and governors.

My children are amused by my tales of what they call "the olden days." They believe me, but cannot totally comprehend a world of farming with mules, houses without plumbing, the harsh reality of what life once was in the mountains. I don't want my children to have to endure an icy February outhouse or to know the humiliation of being labeled; I do wish they could understand—and somehow experience—their heritage.

For the sake of my kids, and others like them—modern youngsters being integrated into the mainstream culture—we need to upgrade the Appalachian image. We're no better, no worse than any other culture. We come from an ancient place, an old society, a region where change didn't come for a long time and then came too fast. We're bridging the gap, adapting to a modern world, but hanging on to our heritage, blessed and cursed by a beautiful but cruel land.

We are, sometimes, our own worst enemy, wanting so desperately to share in America's wealth that we sell out, giving over our land and our culture to people who neither understand nor care about us.

The truth of Appalachia lies between the myths. We are neither "drenched in filth and ignorance" nor a quaint, noble hillfolk; we are people making the best of what we have, becoming better housed, fed, and educated with each decade.

I've grown up with the changes; I liked some and resented others, refused to leave the region, refused to accept the stereotyped statements of who I am. It's time we made some new movies, wrote some accurate books, and put a stop to the mentality that blames a region's problems on human deficiencies.[5]

> I was, at the time the preceding essay was written, on the Berea staff of MATCH, Inc., a humanist effort to organize low-income Appalachian craftspeople, and somehow—unfortunately—I wound up acting as manager for six months of the old Council of the Southern Mountains Appalachian Book and Record Shop. In that capacity I attended the council's annual meeting in Knoxville, Tennessee, and came

home to write about it, to express the mixed opinions of a native son dealing with a regional reality.

It was the seventieth annual meeting of the Council of the Southern Mountains, a small gathering in a neighborhood community center in Knoxville, Tennessee, a time for an observer to compare past with present.

Formed in 1913 as the Conference of Southern Mountain Workers, the council did quiet, solid service to the region for its first forty years, publishing *Mountain Life and Work,* distributing medicine and clothing, coordinating the developing leadership of Appalachia. Longtime director Perly Ayer was one of Appalachia's best-known, best-loved workers, a dedicated and effective leader whose quiet authority set the pace for the organization.

Then the 1960s War on Poverty exploded the council into a multimillion-dollar economic development agency, one with more than forty employees busy crisscrossing the mountains in a frantic battle action, and the council's Berea offices suddenly sprawled over most of the block surrounding the Boone Tavern Hotel.

It was boom time, too much too soon. Perly Ayer died during the hectic years, and a vocal new element began clamoring for a bigger role in the council. Blacks, women, youth, and the poor asked for an equal voice; the dramatic meeting in North Carolina's Fontana Village is often referred to as the "takeover," a proud moment for current leaders and the end of a dream for many of the old-timers.

The council image shifted radically from conservative service to radical activism, a costly changeover in terms of funding. Headquarters were relocated to Clintwood, Virginia, in the heart of the coal country, and the struggle that continues today began.

There is still *Mountain Life and Work,* now an outspoken news magazine with a dwindling circulation, and the Berea-based Appalachian Book and Record Shop clings to existence. But the council's main thrust is now in mine safety, environmental protection, human rights, and other needed but often unpopular public efforts.

By choice, the council is an advocate for Appalachia's poor, a vocal counterpoint to established concepts and philosophy. The controversial stance draws fire; on occasion the fire has literally been gun blasts, directed at council staff members.

So, the seventieth annual meeting did not take place in an elegant resort hotel. Meetings were in the Turnkey III Center, the workplace of council president Almetor King, and many participants spent the night at the center in sleeping bags. There were no three-piece suits—mostly jeans and overalls—and the banquets were communally cooked meals in the center kitchen. All ages were present, gathered to hear reports from the Highlander Center, SOCM (Save Our Cumberland Mountains), the Yellow Creek Concerned Citizens, and other activist programs. Though I personally felt somewhat out of place, I found myself becoming much more understanding of the council's new directions.

I am, definitely, from another world; I don't enjoy sleeping bags on a cement floor, and I'm amused at the number of people who cling so desperately to the 1960s uniforms and slogans. There was a certain wistfulness, a fond remembering of the good old days, a reluctance to accept the fact that the exciting sixties were forever gone. The image and the liturgy were dated, relics of a movement that effectively changed America, and many of those present in Knoxville would do well to accept that reality.

But few people could view the work of the Yellow Creek Concerned Citizens with anything short of admiration for the spunk, concern, good humor, and persistence of those involved. They've raised funds through bake sales, car washes, and private contributions to take their case to Frankfort and Washington, struggling all the way with Middlesboro's bureaucracy and Frankfort's tangled red tape.

I think Perly Ayer would have approved. So would have the early missionaries, the workers who created the Council of the Southern Mountains seventy years ago.

Some of the materials presented at the CSM meeting were the same old tired refrain—the "down-with-the-establishment" tirade—but keen new concerns about resurgent racism, President Reagan's impact on human welfare programs, and the economic future of the region were addressed with real passion.

No "people's" organization can be effective as a professionally organized lobby; CSM addresses publicly unpopular problems with outspoken concern, somehow survives year after year, and even—to the surprise of some—survives the new leadership.

I can't honestly agree with all the views of the council's diverse membership, or even with the staff emphasis on organizing, but I can support the effort and attest to the genuine effort and determination.

I admired the "old" council and wish its direct-service programs could have been preserved.

But the "new" council is much more aware of the problems of the urban Appalachians—the migrants to the larger cities—and much more realistic about the region's population shift to the cities. Knoxville, Charleston, and Pittsburgh are as much a part of Appalachia as are Gimlet and Stinking Creek.

CSM is too much of a single-issue organization, but perhaps that one issue—coal—is the region's dominant factor, the mixed blessing that fuels the economy as it destroys the land and the people.

I'd like to see a reunion, a meeting of the CSM's old and new leadership, to evaluate the status of the region and the agency. I suspect that—once the personal grievances were aired—the two elements would find themselves very much in agreement on many issues.

Both groups, for seventy years, have been primarily concerned with the well-being of Appalachia. Wouldn't a combined effort do more good?[6]

> I declined Jim Wayne Miller's follow-up request that I coordinate a "reunion" of the warring Council of the Southern Mountains factions as part of the Appalachian Studies Association's 1983 conference; by the time Jim asked, I was so weary of the ideological dispute that was to become the council's death struggle that I wanted nothing further to do with any of the clashing personalities and philosophies.
>
> But I wasn't through speaking out, and had taken a position in Morehead State University's Appalachian Development Center to become even more directly involved in the issues and actions concerning the region.

> In 1984 Loyal Jones loaned me a copy of *All That Is Native and Fine,* David Whisnant's controversial new study, and again I felt compelled to write for the *Courier-Journal.*

In his *All That Is Native and Fine,* David Whisnant dares challenge the motives of the many "missionaries" who came to Appalachia from 1890 to 1940 to offer aid and education to the isolated natives. According to Whisnant, such notables as Kathryn Petit, Olive Dame Campbell, Richard Chase, and William J. Hutchins practiced "politics of culture," imposing their own values upon a rural, working-class people.

In his book, which is gradually creating a stir in Appalachian circles, Whisnant suggests that real, early-twentieth-century Appalachian people did not practice English folk dancing or Scandinavian weaving. They preferred, instead, the scandalous banjo, lively clog dancing, and "fotched-on" yard goods.

I cannot personally vouch for pre-1940 preferences, but I suspect Whisnant is mostly correct; I grew up in eastern Kentucky, but never heard a recorder tune or saw a Morris Dance until I came to Berea College in 1961. I did know about Hank Williams and Roy Acuff and the Grand Ole Opry and about a rowdy way of dancing that rattled the rafters and pounded the oiled oak floors.

I was a Berea student before "Appalachian studies" became part of the curriculum, and I stubbornly resented (and resisted) certain faculty efforts to make me over into an acceptable middle-class midwesterner. I still can't say "dead" in a single syllable; I'd still rather listen to Johnny Cash than endure the 175 verses of a plaintive English ballad.

I value the British Isles heritage we all share, but I love the colorful, imperfect personality of the Appalachian culture that evolved from those traditions. And, for all David Whisnant's indignation over the racism, cultural politics, and ignorance of the mountain people of the early 1900s, the settlement schools and social-service agencies served useful roles in education, health, and economic development.

The condescendingly stubborn missionaries failed in their efforts to block the impact of radios, cars, and mail-order catalogs;

our culture went its own way despite their righteous protests and cultural politics.

And, perhaps unintentionally, the schools and agencies played a vital role in overcoming the mountain isolation. Youngsters trained at Hindman and Pine Mountain and Berea came home to build the school systems, hospitals, highways, electrical cooperatives, and communications networks that brought the outside world to the fingertips of every Appalachian.

Maybe the settlement schools would have preferred to educate only those students considered "native and fine," but their classrooms were open to young banjo pickers and clog dancers and hillbilly singers. As it turns out, the banjo is not nearly so immoral as it was once assumed to be.

Whisnant is also critical of those involved in the early Appalachian handcraft revival. Berea College, he says, imposed Scandinavian designs upon local weavers (Whisnant doesn't even acknowledge the New England furniture designs of Wallace Nutting, which are still the backbone of Berea's furniture production).

Whisnant accuses the region's craft leaders of overemphasis on art, as opposed to native talent, of designing non-Appalachian goods for sale in an urban marketplace.

He's right again—partly. Most Appalachian crafts were once marketed outside the region; today, tourists are the prime customers. So-called "designer-craftsmen" do dominate the craft organizations, and home-trained, native craftspeople are rare.

But the traditional quilts, baskets, cornshuck dolls, and wooden toys are today produced in record numbers; the workplace may now be a mobile home instead of a cabin, and the producer may be a college graduate, but the products are largely unchanged.

Perhaps the crafts are no longer "native and fine," and the old romance is missing. But had not Berea College and the Southern Highland Handicraft Guild worked so hard, there would be nothing. As it is, a multimillion-dollar industry is thriving.

The early mountain workers were almost universally shocked by the conditions they found in Appalachia, and they drew some absurd, condescending conclusions, often mistaking isolation and ignorance for lack of intelligence.

Perhaps, in more accurate hindsight, the truth is as simple as that the missionaries were as ignorant of us as we were of them. And, having personally known many of the dedicated "outsiders" who worked so hard to help, my judgments are less harsh.

In 1965 I went to Asheville, North Carolina, to join the staff of the venerable Southern Highland Handicraft Guild. My first assignment was to read Allen Eaton's 1937 book *Handicrafts of the Southern Highlands,* an 1890-to-1930 history of the Appalachian handcraft revival. In less than two months, I'd met many of the people Eaton wrote about: gentle Clementine Douglas, Campbell Folk School director Marguerite Bidstrup, Tennessee woodworker O. J. Mattil, Penland School director Miss Lucy Morgan, Berea's Helen Dingman, and former guild director Louise Pitman.

Never, anywhere, have I met people more caring and giving. If they were typical of those who had such an impact on our mountain culture, we should perhaps pray for a new wave.

But contemporary Appalachia is not really a land of dulcimer players, Maypole dancers, and coverlet weavers, no more than it is a land of welfare addicts, incestuous defectives, and moonshine runners.

Neither the romantic nor the cynical view is absolutely right or wrong.

We're a lot livelier than the folklorists would have you believe, and, as Whisnant points out, we drive Camaros, shop at K-mart, and watch too much television—just like people anywhere else.[7]

> My last appearance in "Your Turn" was when another Appalachian book became a movie, when Jane Fonda—of all people, "Hanoi Jane"—played in *The Dollmaker.*

Thirty years after its successful publication, Harriette Simpson Arnow's classic Appalachian novel *The Dollmaker* finally came to the TV screen (last Sunday on ABC) and—except for a contrived happy ending—Jane Fonda and company did a surprisingly good job.

The scenic backdrops (Tennessee, not Kentucky), picturesque cabins, and vintage vehicles were a mite too glossy, and some of the characters seemed to have been carved from mountain hardwoods, but, all in all, *The Dollmaker* offered a positive, fairly authentic portrayal of Appalachia, light years better than most previous efforts to capture the mountain lifestyle on film.

Fonda was good, not great. But the finest performance was turned in by Levon Helm as tinkering Clovis Nevels, the dollmaker's husband.

The combination of arrogance and ignorance (read "lack of knowledge," not lack of intelligence) reflected in his character was very real, very painful to those of us who were children of the mountain men who so desperately wanted a better life during and immediately after World War II.

Depressing as the movie may have been (to those who haven't read Arnow's book), the living conditions depicted were a sanitized, middle-class version of the way it really was; neither Appalachian Kentucky nor housing-project Detroit were so bright and cheerful.

Perhaps the new, happy ending was necessary for television, but victory—and the return to Kentucky—blunted the dismal, powerful ending that Harriette Arnow wrote.

The book ends with despair and hopelessness, a far more realistic depiction of the way it really was for the mountain families who migrated north.

The truth is that most migrants never came home, except for weekends and funerals and family reunions. Today, a fourth generation of Appalachian migrants is being born in Cincinnati, Detroit, and South Bend; a generation of ghetto and suburb residents who will never see the hills of Kentucky except as they drive down I-75 en route to the Great Smoky Mountains and Disneyworld. Greyhound no longer runs its legendary Friday night "Appalachian Express," even though the massive traffic jam every Friday night in Cincinnati attests that many still make the trip back home weekly.

The other reality is that most of those who do come home—for a Sunday dinner of chicken and dumplings and a trunkload of canned green beans and fresh pulled corn—don't ever want to move back. They are now children of the city, factory workers and suburban landowners, with offspring who sneer at the slower pace of small town Kentucky.

When I discovered *The Dollmaker* in 1962, I sat up all night reading. I wept with Gertie Nevels, but I also rejoiced at the discovery of a writer who truly knew the Appalachian people. Harriette Arnow's fiction is filled with hard-to-read dialect for those not familiar with the language, and her work neither glorifies nor condemns the mountain culture. Both *Hunter's Horn* and *The Dollmaker* deal with Appalachian families adjusting from self-sufficient isolation to the encroaching modern world.

I was part of that adjustment. After World War II, most of my family scattered away from Elliott County to the factories of Youngstown, Mansfield, and Cleveland; we went only a few miles, to a Fleming County tenant farm, and made the trip from Bluebank back to Gimlet every Sunday morning.

My Ohio cousins would come for their brief visits, calling for "Mother" instead of "Mommy," saying "isn't" instead of "ain't," bearing fascinating tales of supermarkets, theaters, and colorful city personalities. They were immediately, smugly superior to us country cousins.

Now my far-flung cousins and I are middle-aged observers, they in industrial Ohio and I here in Morehead. By the time I was finally able to taste their modern conveniences and bustling city lifestyle, I was already too set in my ways, too attuned to life in the hills to make a switch.

I suspect that folklorists disapprove of Harriette Arnow as much as they do of me and my writing; Arnow accurately chronicles Appalachia's adjustment to the twentieth century, understands the desire of the young people to see and sample the "outside" world, and writes about firsthand reality instead of about romantic dulcimer pluckers and Maypole dancers.

Jane Fonda brought *The Dollmaker* to life as well as could be expected, with a loving attention to detail to be much admired. The book, with its dismal story line but with characters strong and enduring, is much better.[8]

> The "Your Turn" era of my life led to much more writing—book reviews for controversial *Courier-Journal* book editor Sally Bingham, reviews of Appalachian books for other publications, and even a short stint as a dues-paying member of the National Book Critics Circle.

My career as a literary reviewer screeched to a halt when—with encouragement from Sally Bingham—I called Olive Ann Burns's *Cold Sassy Tree* "stock, stereotypical Southern corn. It may well be the worst 'Southern' novel ever written. It is demeaning, racist, and dull."

Back came a letter to Ms. Bingham from Charles Boswell of Heineken and Associates, Ltd., a sales rep for Ticknor and Fields, calling my review "vituperative drivel" and saying that I wouldn't have been able to recognize the literary merit of Mark Twain's *Huckleberry Finn*.[9]

Copies of the vituperative letter sent to two Louisville bookstores added another subtle message: don't sell Garry Barker's books.

While I still don't rank *Cold Sassy Tree* up with *Huckleberry Finn* (or even with *Scarlett*), I've regretted the review from the second it appeared in print. I was guilty of critical smugness, of looking for bad things to say. Having been at the receiving end of similar snobbish reviews, I know how it feels.

So, in 1984, I removed myself from the National Book Critics Circle and from active book reviewing.

But the "Your Turn" sequence was rich training for me, at once a heady and painful experience, good preparation for what lay ahead.

A Generation of "In-betweeners"

This 1983 essay from *Southern Exposure* helped define me and my directions, pinpointing for perhaps the first time my feelings of not being a part of either end of the extremes of Appalachian life, of the frustrations and mixed emotions of being caught squarely in the middle.

We're the teachers, bankers, journalists, attorneys, doctors, and merchants—the "war babies" of the early 1940s who are best described as Appalachian "in-betweeners." We're too young to be traditional mountaineers, too old to accept a radical line of thinking.

We were the last generation to grow up before LBJ's War on Poverty brought new expectations to Appalachia; we are conservative liberals, embracing tradition and futurism, young middle-aged workers who've seen our homeland cram a century of progress into three decades.

We grew up in a rigid world with clearly defined values. "Give a day's work for a day's pay." "Go to school, work hard, accept responsibility."

My Berea College classmates were intelligent, committed, stubbornly determined to break away from poverty. Many of us were the first from our families to attend college, or even to graduate from high school. We were at Berea because we were poor and Berea was cheap. We were a conservative lot, products of a heritage that decreed that brains plus hard work equaled success.

The early 1960s Civil Rights movement distressed me; I was in total sympathy, but could not—then—offer much more. I was too wrapped up in my own struggles, too aware of the problems of my own people, and—frankly—very skeptical of passive protest.

Even Vietnam, at first, was simple. My country was at war, right or wrong. My break from tradition came shortly. My friends were killed, the survivors deeply scarred, and then my draft board requested the pleasure of my company.

They should have called two years sooner. My newborn son kept me free. I felt guilty, confused, and angry, torn between my warlike heritage and a disgust with our government for fighting a senseless, political war.

At home, I watched the War on Poverty and again couldn't tell who was winning. I was thrilled with the new highways and hospitals, but appalled at the waste in many projects.

A horde of well-meaning young people descended upon us, full of ideas and expectations but woefully short on administrative ability and common sense. It was high adventure: challenging the power structure, rattling across ridgetops in four-wheel-drive Scouts, shocking the unprepared mountaineers.

The legions of LBJ's army swept in with federal cash and lofty ideals. Most of the ideals—and some of the workers—were beaten back by the mountains and the problems, but the battle signaled a new way of life in Appalachia.

I admired the intense effort, shuddered at the naive approach, fumed at the degrading image sent to the "outside" world. I had one foot in the past and one in the future; I was acceptable to neither the old-timers nor the outsiders, and that's where I still stand after nearly twenty years of working here.

I suspect I'm not alone. I'm neither hidebound traditionalist nor screaming radical, neither ashamed of Appalachia's progress nor totally satisfied. I'm proud of all we've done, but I want more. I have fond memories of growing up poor, but I don't want my children to endure the same. Some of the old ways are best left to the history books, but some of the new ways offend me.

I have problems with our massive assistance program. No person should go cold or hungry and everyone deserves proper medical care and sanitary housing, but I detest penalizing people who want to work. The people I grew up with who accepted welfare did so grudgingly. Now some find it to be a rewarding profession.

Many changes are for the better. The physical improvements—

bathrooms and highways and telephones—have eased the burden of life in Appalachia; there is also a greater tolerance of individual differences, acceptance of those who would choose new ways of thinking, a loosening of religious controls.

Yet I still admire the old-time values. I loved the old, solid family unit, the sense of community and willingness to do whatever needed doing. Respect for elders, enjoying life without gadgets or stimulants, determined self-sufficiency—these seem to have been discarded, replaced by the "me" generation, by video games, Valium, impersonal sex, and an attitude that even those who don't make an effort deserve public support.

We in-betweeners are bridging the gap between old and new, quietly moving forward. We haven't been publicized, but we're here, doing the things that have to be done.

In 1965 I asked my boss—Southern Highland Handicraft Guild director Robert Gray—how we could affect lasting change in the mountains. His answer was blunt and simple. Educate native leaders, keep them in the region, and wait. Let the people solve their own problems. It's happening, slowly but surely, and the process is changing the face of Appalachia, forever eliminating our isolation from and ignorance of the ways of the outside world.

I wish it would move faster; I wish it would slow down. I want improvement, but I'm reluctant to see the Appalachian heritage absorbed into the American melting pot.

I'm afraid we in-betweeners are the last of a breed, the final generation to have intimately known the old mountain ways. We lived what our children study as history; we have adapted, adjusted, and survived the rapid change.

We are what "they" say Appalachia does not have. We are, essentially, the newly born middle class, the people who do the work, pay the taxes, and provide the stability. We're beginning to be the government, the "traditional" leadership, the people who will guide the region for the next thirty years.

When it's time, we'll hand it over to our children and their children with, I hope, a sense of history allowing us to accept the changes they will make. I likely will disagree with their ideas, tell them so, but admire their determination to do it their own way.[10]

> Ten years later I resurrected the aging "in-betweeners" essay as part of the text for the 1992 art/essay book *Mitchell Tolle: American Artist,* a collaborative effort with the Lewis County, Kentucky, native whose superb artwork earns national acclaim and whose marketing firm, Painted Treasures, Inc., is taking the selling of art one major step forward.
>
> In the new book, some old concepts took new forms; some long studied ideas came into a clearer focus.
>
> For example, this chapter opening is a blunt, matter-of-fact, condensed, and highly personal history of the region.

I come from the Kentucky mountains.

From a mixed and misunderstood heritage of beauty and sometimes brutal violence, from abject poverty set ironically amidst nature's grandest splendor, from a proud and self-sufficient people who've endured two centuries of stereotype, ridicule, and a widespread public lack of understanding of the strength and character that draw upon a deep-rooted and lasting heritage.

I've been called a hillbilly, a hick, a redneck, a briar, a "contemporary ancestor," an Appalachian. I've been called "close to the earth," "quaint," "stoic," and lots of other labels, good and bad, used over the years in an attempt to sum up a diverse culture, geography, economy, and personality in one easy word.

Appalachia is mules and moonshine, square dances and story-songs, pickup trucks and sharp-shooting riflemen, but it is much, much more. We should be equally renowned for our faith, loyalty, resourcefulness, our overriding sense of fair play, and our inborn awareness of the necessity to coexist with nature and live in harmony with the forces that help shape the way we are.

Appalachia's early settlers were a private, self-sufficient, God-fearing band of pioneers of mostly Scotch-Irish descent, men and women determined to live free, to live from and with the land, to work and worship however they chose.

That independent, isolated lifestyle was to last, largely untouched, well into this century, though the Civil War brought much personal and economic hardship to the region, and in the bitter aftermath of feuds and deprivation much of the educational system was lost. The last half of the nineteenth century was, in much of Appalachia, a bleak period when a remote culture became even more removed from the rest of America.

But missionaries, economics, and world wars were to forever break down the old barriers and open up the mountains to the dramatic changes.

Appalachia's plentiful timber and coal drew the money-makers, corporate moguls who grabbed up logging and mineral rights from trusting mountaineers and harvested the natural bounty with little regard for the people or for their lands.

Christian missionaries brought improved education and health care to Appalachia, established settlement schools, churches, and the "nurses on horseback" of the Frontier Nursing Service; the missionary effort drew much attention to the mountain culture, the music, crafts, and folkways so primitive to the rest of the world.

As better roads and electricity filtered into Appalachia, the traditional economy based on the barter system began to give way to a cash economy; money was used to order the goods by mail that once were woven, spun, forged, carved, and made by hand from available materials to fill everyday needs.

Modernized coal camps sprang up near the mines, and outside workers were recruited to help go under ground and bring out the "black gold."

The "war to end all wars," World War I, changed Appalachia's culture and took young fighting men off the farms and into the training camps, into the cities and across the Atlantic on troopships, to the battlefields of France, and—for many—to simple graves far from their sheltering mountains.

In Tennessee and North Carolina the Tennessee Valley Authority (TVA) and the Great Smoky Mountains National Park brought progress at the expense of uprooted families. The TVA electricity triggered much industrial growth; the new lakes and national park brought tourism to Tennessee; but always the more remote mountain pockets were left largely untouched.

The Great Depression had a comparatively less impact on the mountains; an already hard life got harder, and an enduring people simply survived one more difficult challenge. The Works Progress

Administration (WPA) and Civilian Conservation Corps (CCC) created work for many young mountain men, and for many opened the doors to an out-migration that still drains the region.

World War II reached into every mountain family and community. Many of the young men and women who didn't serve in active military duty left instead for the war industries in the larger northern cities.

Many—both the soldiers and the industrial workers—did not return to their mountain homes. Whole families migrated to jobs in the North—in Detroit, Dayton, Cleveland, Cincinnati, and Indianapolis—and created pockets of transplanted Appalachia in those cities.[11]

> An equally simplistic view of mountain music, written from the heart, not the head, for the same book, pleases me.

From the Grand Ole Opry stage to the back porch fiddle and guitar, the music of the mountains tells the stories, celebrates the sweet sounds, draws out the heart and soul of those who live through sound and rhythm.

The fiddle is a bagpipe with strings, a resined bow alive and dancing in deft, skilled hands, a worn wooden box tucked neatly between chin and shoulder, a tiny instrument that can give voice to a shriek or a cackle, a train whistle, a happy jig, or the plaintive mourn of a winter wind rustling softly across a lonesome mountaintop.

The fiddle and the banjo, and the music played over the radio, were evil personified to many of the missionary ladies who brought better education to Appalachia. The lively instruments of the devil were corrupting a culture, leading young mountain men and women astray into lives of music and moonshine, killing off the traditional ballads so loved by the collectors who raced frantically through the fertile hills trying to find and document the undiluted purity before somebody else got there first.

As it turned out, banjo and fiddle players weren't altogether devilish, and the mission schools *did* open their doors to the young fiddlers, so both the ballads and the bluegrass are alive and well today.

Everywhere in the mountains there is music. High school bands with blaring trumpets, all-night gospel sings in crowded auditoriums, country music stars in sparkly sequins and gaudy cars, balladeers and singers of old-timey songs, young guitar pickers with Nashville on their minds.

Jean Ritchie's true clear voice, Loretta Lynn's tribute to the coal miner's daughter, the driving bluegrass sounds of Ricky Skaggs, and even the new-era electric sounds of the Kentucky Headhunters draw on a heritage of singing and picking just for fun, on back porch and living room jam sessions, on the sheer joy and necessity of making music.

Wilma Dykeman wrote about the mountain music maker who once said "I'm a fiddler, you know. Not a violinist. What I play is old time stuff. I don't know a thing about music."[12] The point was that his music was not a separate part of the mountain man's life; it was as nourishing and necessary as daily bread.[13]

> And the final chapter of *Mitchell Tolle: American Artist* expresses my concern that our heritage is not being passed on down as it should be, as it would be if we all believed it was actually worth the effort.

The strong sense of family, of the past living in the present and on into the future through close generational ties, is a dominant factor in the Appalachian heritage and in our everyday life.

We honor the elderly, those who've endured and labored so that younger generations might enjoy the fruits of progress, and often our closest ties are to the grandparents, even great-grandparents, to those who represent living ties to history, to family roots, to a personal sense of place and of belonging.

The first question I was most likely to be asked when I was growing up and met a new person was "Whose boy are you?" The genealogy and the location of the specific mountain, creek, hollow, or crossroads a particular family called home helped to establish a kinship, sometimes literally, that would be the basis for an unspoken trust and understanding.

"I know your people, therefore I know you" was and is the

common thread in every Appalachian life; it expresses the instinctive need to build a relationship more personal than a handshake, more meaningful than a formal introduction.

And, it often seems, the farther we are removed from the homeplace, from the immediate family, the more important is the recognition of those strong ties to place and to people.

If two eastern Kentuckians meet in New York, Los Angeles, London, or Tokyo, there is the immediate "Who are you and where are you from?" preliminary to determine just how quickly and how closely personal bonds will be formed.

When we live or travel away from the region, nothing ever feels quite so good, so right, as to meet somebody from "back home," someone whose basic culture and values don't have to be explained or explored.

Much of what we are, what we know, and what we believe has been passed down to us through the generations as living history, oral history, a culture preserved by a strong tradition of storytelling, songs, and a need to share the lesson of the past with those who will be the future.

As a child I clung to every word my grandfathers offered, and now—a grandfather myself—I understand even better the need to ensure that another generation learns its heritage. I feel a deep need to share family history and folklore with my grandsons, a sharing my own son may have partially missed, because when he was small I was too busy, too caught up in trying to get ahead and help change our present, to worry about the past.

But my children had my parents as guides, and that's part of what grandparents are for, part of the privilege and obligation we assume as keepers of the family traditions.

And, with every generation, those traditions are weakened as we move farther out into the world and as that same world more easily comes into our mountain homes.

Our young people today have ready access to a world that did not exist in the Appalachia of just forty years ago, to televisions and computers, to high-tech consolidated schools and to shopping malls; they have easy access to cities and the larger world outside the hills and to a lifestyle largely freed from the daily chores that were once a necessary part of every family's survival.

As a group we—the older generation—are guilty of overlooking a basic part of our youngsters' educations, and that is in the teaching of our very own history, our culture and heritage, our distinct difference. We have all been, perhaps, too busy enacting changes and speeding up the progress to stop and realize that our own heritage is in danger of slipping away.

Most of our schools do not teach Appalachian history and literature, do not foster a sense of value of the traditional ways, and do not honor that which helped shape us all.

We tend to overlook our own artists, writers, musicians, storytellers, craftspeople, and characters to study instead those same influences and histories shared by the rest of the world.

Somewhat ironically, scholars and teachers from outside the region do study and teach about us and our history, and often elementary school students from metropolitan Louisville learn more about the Appalachian culture than do the children who live here.

While others elsewhere are being taught to value mountain heritage and folklore, those of us who are natives have lived our lives with an ever-present message, sometimes subtle but often bluntly painful, that to be Appalachian is to be less than equal. We have been told for two hundred years to discard our beliefs, our accents, our ingrown ways, and our traditional concepts, to cast aside our heritage and adjust to modern America.[14]

Slings and Arrows

I guess it had to finally happen.

I made the homefolks mad, in spades, and set off a painful year of bitter recrimination that still lies uneasy just below the surface.

I wrote "Home Again" and chose to publish it in *Appalachian Heritage* to make sure the essay did not get misunderstood and sensationalized, figuring that the readers of a literary quarterly devoted to the region would know how to take my words.

I was right and wrong.

Nothing I've ever written triggered more responses, either way, than did "Home Again."

First came an outpouring of tears, congratulations, and admiration from subscribers for the power and simplicity of the piece.

Then the other shoe dropped.

A librarian photocopied "Home Again," and a mass circulation within Elliott County seems to have reached every household. Angry letters, phone calls, and visitors suddenly descended upon *Appalachian Heritage* editor Sidney Farr, demanding retractions and apologies; full-front page coverage in the *Elliott County News* (including my open letter of apology) caught the interest of the *Lexington Herald-Leader,* and their article fanned the already hot flames.

Reporter Todd Pack wrote, in part:

> The essay, "Home Again," published in the February issue of *Appalachian Heritage,* has been talked about across lunch

> counters and elsewhere since photocopies surfaced here two weeks ago, said Wanda Oliver, director of the county library.
>
> "I haven't heard anybody say anything good about it," she said.
>
> "Maybe he didn't mean to put the people down, but I don't think he should have said the things he said," said Faye Whitley, editor of the *Elliott County News.*
>
> Several people said they thought he [Barker] was bragging about his education and the fact he could go to places like New York.
>
> "If he thinks he's the only one from here who ever went to college," said Wilma Hutchinson, the county bookmobile librarian. "How does he think we got all these teachers and lawyers?"
>
> Barker, who left Elliott County when he was 5, said he was not trying to belittle or brag.
>
> "I wrote it to get rid of my frustrations," he said. "I was a little reluctant to publish this. I didn't want it to have a wide circulation who might misinterpret it."
>
> Barker, however, said he could understand why some people did not like what he wrote. "In some ways," he said, "the truth hurts."[15]

The hurt spread quickly. My books were promptly removed from the Elliott County Library. One outraged cousin made the trip to Berea to lodge a personal protest; another wrote an angry, bitter letter, the only letter I answered.

But other letters poured in. Letters so full of hate, twisted resentment, and promised biblical and physical revenge that I stopped even reading them, stopped responding in any way.

My family—my parents, brothers and sisters, nieces—were caught in the middle, not at all part of what I'd written but instinctively coming to my defense.

My aunt and uncle, parents of the two young men killed in a blasting accident, probably suffered the most, a fact that never leaves my mind. That never will leave my mind. Unintentionally, I hurt two people very dear to me and somehow dragged them into a controversy that seemingly will not go away.

I asked a Berea student from Elliott County to read

"Home Again" and respond. She understood both sides of the battle. My point of view, she said, was that of a native once removed. Or, as *Elliott County News* editor Faye Whitley put it, "Mr. Barker . . . has been gone from the mountains too long."

Ms. Whitley's written assessment of my essay was that it was "[a] harsh description. Too harsh, too one-sided, unmindful of the myriad of pleasant, progressive aspects of the county, of the independence, self sufficiency and hospitality of our people, most of whom are as honest and progressive as any people anywhere."[16]

An eloquent assessment.

My own letter of apology, run on the front page with the article, read, in part:

> I didn't come back last September as a reporter. I came to Sandy Hook because my mother was so upset when she called to tell me about the three tragic deaths, because I felt a need to show my support for the survivors. I wasn't paid to write for *Appalachian Heritage,* and didn't come looking for a story.
>
> And I didn't write a news story. I am a writer who, as James Still says, must write out my frustrations and feelings. I wrote the "Home Again" essay not as objective journalism but as an emotional, from-the-heart expression of frustration over the deaths of three young people.
>
> I wrote fleeting impressions, distorted by emotion, not objective facts. I did not intend to add to the grief. Anyone who knows me also knows that I would never deliberately hurt anyone or anything, ever, for any reason.
>
> I am fully aware that there are many good things about life in Elliott County, that what I presented was a very narrow vision distorted by the situation.
>
> To all of you, I again apologize. My naive good intentions were in error, and I'm very sorry. My words have caused pain, and that causes pain for me.[17]

A follow-up call, from a cousin, pointed out, angrily, that in my letter I said was sorry but didn't say I was wrong.

That's true.

I have, since 1990, reread "Home Again" probably one hundred times.

With, still, very mixed emotions.

It is a harsh criticism, made intensely personal by the fact that it was written by a native son. The same essay, from an outside writer, would have triggered healthy anger and resentment; coming from me, it was a traitorous indictment. Heresy.

It is true, perhaps, that I've been gone from that particular part of the mountains too long, that my education and experience have removed me from my roots.

I don't know.

Read and judge for yourself:

Life is still hard in the remote, rugged hills of Elliott County, Kentucky.

Unemployment is chronic, Kentucky's highest at 25 percent and more; there are no industries, no significant coal deposits, little flat land for profitable farming. The sparse population, impossible terrain, financially strapped government and school systems, and politics—the sheriff who doesn't work, the tax assessor who doesn't mail out the bills—keep the county underdeveloped and in the Lexington news. A mass exodus over the past fifty years has weakened the pool of homegrown talent and leadership, and further handicapped this forgotten little pocket of Kentucky.

Tobacco crops are cultivated on steep hillsides better suited to growing marijuana, probably today's number one cash crop in the county. Most who do have jobs commute. To nearby Morehead, to Ashland, to the West Virginia coal mines, even to Lexington, a hard two-hour drive away.

My family is from Gimlet, on Mauk Ridge in Elliott County, but few of us still live there. Most migrated out after World War II, north to the Ohio factories. We moved, when I was about three years old, forty miles west to relatively flat and prosperous Fleming County. But we went home, every Sunday, to Elliott County, and I spent my summers there until I was too big to be spared so long from farm work, and Elliott County has held a special place in my memories all these years, a place where I have a special feeling for home, heritage, and family.

I went back to Elliott County on a September Tuesday for a triple funeral, two young first cousins and a wife, killed while trying to blast open an old spring-fed well to get water to a mobile home. The first was killed by poison gas; the other two died in vain rescue attempts.

Even in the Kentucky mountains, death is steady work. Probably the newest and nicest building in Sandy Hook, the county seat of Elliott County, is the funeral home. Modern, immaculate, brick-veneered, surrounded by a huge paved parking lot, air conditioned, the facility for leaving this world is far superior to any facility for being born.

The crowd gathers early. The men come in dress cowboy boots, jeans or cheap dress pants, plaid flannel shirts, or cowboy-cut uniform shirts; they have the raw and uncomfortable dressed-up look of loggers, truckers, and farmers. The women are too old for their years, worn by hard work, childbirth, poor medical care, and a lifestyle that leaves little room for frills.

Some of the younger women are beautiful in a classic mountain way. High cheekbones, fair skin, light hair, and clear blue eyes reflect the Cox family genes—my mother's blood, the Irish heritage that still surfaces.

The older people are stiff, slowed, uncomplaining, grimly accepting of the tragedy. They accept me too, despite my jacket, tie, and uncalloused hands, once they ask and discover I'm Hack and Loval's second boy, the one who went away to college.

The service is in the hands of the brothers, leaders of the family church—a dozen of them seated near the coffins—but first there's a surprising guitar-accompanied duet of a popular gospel song. Probably, we decide later, the young surviving wife insisted on this music and had her way despite the brothers' ban on musical instruments. Then there's the undertaker's brief and formal summary of three short lives, and the brothers take over.

Their music is a cappella, lined out by the leader, and the hill country's version of a Gregorian chant fills the overcrowded parlor with a strangely harmonic, emotional, and primitive beauty.

The first brother then takes the floor, speaking softly at first, warming up, breaking out in a sweat, building, then suddenly he bursts into his hellfire and damnation Sunday sermon. For this is, to my outsider's surprise, a sermon. For the first half hour or so there is a certain basic beauty and meaning to the rhythmic chanting, and many in the congregation add their vocal support.

The second and third brothers to preach don't fare so well, from an audience point of view. Women wander out to change diapers and nurse babies. Men step outside to smoke and talk crops. We all sweat, stiffen, and take advantage of the lull to inspect each other.

We number probably two hundred family, friends, neighbors, and morbid sightseers. Maybe half the hundred or so first cousins are here; though many of us are personal strangers, we are drawn by family ties and mountain tradition. I try to recognize family branches, to sort out the Cox and Skaggs families, to recall the cousins, aunts, and uncles I once shared these hillsides with forty years ago.

Halfway through the third brother's sermon, the funeral director is trying to stay on schedule. The brother sees the signals and responds. "I'll hush up soon," he says, then goes on as planned. There are deputy sheriffs and Kentucky state police outside, as arranged, to direct traffic. A Lexington TV crew is waiting at one of the family graveyards.

Finally, the last brother leads the ending chant.

Apologetically, the funeral director explains a complicated viewing procedure brought about by the huge crowd. "I wish we could do better," he offers lamely. We line up and file through, shake hands with the brothers and my uncle, then exit, as directed, through the side door.

Outside in the sunshine, cigarettes are lit. My Uncle Nelson still rolls his own from Prince Albert. I meet curious cousins, anxious to find out if my different life on a faraway college campus has changed me, and they're relieved to find out that I still don't talk proper, that I remember our childhood games and play-places, that I haven't forgotten where I come from. I deliver a set of my books to an uncle only a year or two older than I am. The tiny aunt who delivered me in 1943 looks up, big-eyed, wondering out loud how such a little bitty baby got to be so tall.

I tower over most of the crowd. The Elliott County Coxes are mostly short, fair-skinned people, and only the Barker branch turned out tall, dark-skinned, long-nosed children.

We look for my father, find him in my sister's car, bring him slowly up to shake hands with my uncle. The two old veterans, close friends since childhood, share without speaking.

Three sets of young pallbearers bring out three coffins. Police and funeral home personnel direct traffic, and finally the crush of trucks and cars lines out to begin the winding journey to the two hilltop family graveyards. We drop out of the procession when it turns toward Newfoundland Gap. My father rides with me to Morehead, where we will meet my sisters and mother.

Daddy tries to explain why he suddenly felt weak and dizzy and sat in the car during the service. He blames the heat, his bad back, his age. We both know it was emotion, the kind he cannot openly express.

He recalls the last time he was in Sandy Hook, in 1943, to enlist in the navy just after I was born. We talk about preachers and religion, and agree that a service that makes you angry is better skipped, and that all religions are good until they get to fighting about which one is the best. In Morehead we go to a fast-food restaurant, the first one my father's ever been in, and to his surprise he likes the chicken sandwich.

From Morehead it's eighty miles home for me, on interstate highways that split easily through the hills, with the Olds set on cruise control and the air conditioner purring: for almost two hours I drive and try to sort out emotions.

I am angry. Three young people are dead because economic development programs ignore the remote areas. It is expensive to run water lines across steep ridges, but if there had been a line to that hilltop my cousins would still be alive. I'm angry that life is still so hard in Elliott County, that life is still so cheap, that children there must grow up without all the things that most of us now take for granted.

But, at the same time, I'm curiously envious of the ones of our family who stayed in Elliott County, those who endure and maintain, who bring the slow progress, who live on the same lands our family helped settle. I wonder, as I drive, how my life would have been if we hadn't left Gimlet: surely there'd be no computers to maintain, no monthly sales reports, no committee meetings, no jet travel and plastic hotel rooms, no daily pressures to court customers, cut costs, or count inventories.

Maybe.

I'll never know.

I decide, finally, that I have the best of both worlds: a mountain heritage and a modern lifestyle. And I can always go home, no matter what, to a place where roots run deep and family loyalty rules over all else. Comforted, I take the Berea exit off busy I-75.

The week following the triple funeral at Sandy Hook I travel to the lush rolling farmlands and sprawling metropolis of Nashville, Tennessee, and then on to the Manhattan skyscrapers of New York City. In neither city do the residents have to blast out old wells to get water. Two nights in the New York Helmsley cost about five hundred dollars. There's a phone in the bathroom and a maid to turn down the bedcovers at night.

The whole time I'm in New York, I have this distracting thought: for what it cost the Washington-based agency to bring me here, for a ten-minute presentation, a new water line could have been run to that remote Elliott County hilltop.[18]

> Late in 1993, *Appalachian Heritage* published "Gone Too Long," my belated follow-up to "Home Again," and there were minor repercussions, valid arguments that some of what I wrote would have been better left unsaid.
>
> But parts of the new essay did need saying, not to Elliott County but to those of us who write about Appalachia.

I won't go home again to set off more bitterness. I want to go; I know we should all take an open, honest look at our differences.

We won't.

That's not the way it works, in real life, in families and communities removed from the sphere of academics. My kinfolks and I will never openly discuss my essay, my removal from the culture I treasure but can't share on a day-to-day basis.

Ironically, I suffer often from the very same stubborn pride I tend to criticize in print, from the angry indignation of being considered less than civilized, less than equal.

But Faye Whitley was correct, about me and about lots of you, when she wrote in 1990 that I'd been "gone far too long from the mountains."

How many of the people who regularly write about Appalachia really *know,* from intimate, everyday contact, how the people they're writing about really feel and really live? How many write from memory and from surface impressions? How many rely on statistics, interviews with handpicked representatives, and what other writers have written?

I *know* how it feels to have grown up poor in rural Appalachia. I'm either blessed or handicapped, depending on your point of view, by the old scars, strengths, insights, and single-sightedness of that experience.

I do *not* know how it feels to be growing up today in the very same places, in the very same families. At age fifty I'm still coming to grips with my contradictory life experiences, still wondering if I really belong in either world.

What I want, and can't have, is equal access. The best of both worlds.

I'll continue to write about the quest.

But I now write with my eyes opened, with the knowledge that I have, indeed, been "gone far too long."[19]

> Even before "Gone Too Long" was in print, Elliott County extension agent Gwenda Adkins called. Would I, she asked, meet with and help the publicity committee of the new Elliott County Tourism Development Council?
>
> "Are you sure it's *me* you want?" I asked.
>
> I do have a strong life wish.
>
> She convinced me, and a few weeks later I made a nervous trip home again. One immediate result was this "Appalachian Voices" column on the new economic development project for the *Lexington Herald-Leader.*

There is no more beautiful scenic drive, in all of Appalachia, than to wind slowly across the meandering mountain roadway from Morehead to Sandy Hook.

Sheer cliffs, rolling mountaintops, manicured hillside farmlands, and the dramatic sudden drop down into the Little Sandy River Gorge, on a late October morning under sparkling sunshine, are a spiritual experience, an affirmation of the strength and beauty of the Kentucky mountains, an ironically deceptive sense of prosperity and plenty.

The same trip, on a dreary, drizzly February morning, would be an entirely different experience, a grim and sobering reminder that these same rugged hills—despite the presence of some new, palatial houses—are home to Kentucky's highest unemployment rate, a grinding population drain, and a stagnated economy that offers no hope to the county's young people except to follow the same road back to the outside.

Half the county's current working population now commutes to neighboring counties—even to neighboring states—for employment, and the young residents who do finish college are forced to look elsewhere for careers.

But now there's new life stirring in the Elliott County hills, local leadership with a plan to use the natural bounty to create economic activity.

Construction is scheduled to begin in 1995 on a new twelve-hundred-foot suspension bridge spanning the Laurel Cliffs and on a bypass around Sandy Hook. The new Elliott County Tourism Development Council proposes to make good use of the old road, the Little Sandy Gorge, and the Laurel Creek Gorge.

The plan is ambitious. Hiking, camping, horseback riding, and the natural beauty and historical significance of the gorges are the primary attractions, but local leaders envision more: the Laurel Appalachian Community Center will be a multipurpose facility including the two-thousand-seat Keith Whitley Memorial Music Hall, an outdoor amphitheater, and a regional conference/exhibition/performance site that anchors the development.

The county's much-celebrated and nationally recognized folk artists are another key element, and a "folk art village"—studios and retail shops—would be built along the existing roadway.

The entire project would be managed by a citizens' board as an arm of the fiscal court, with a strong awareness of the necessity for environmental stability and historical preservation. Development is contingent upon cooperation from the U.S. Corps of Engineers and developmental funding from various state and federal agencies.

That cooperation and funding are long overdue, a sign of much-deserved recognition for a community that has decided to lift itself into the next century.

We are all accustomed to hearing the bad news from eastern Kentucky—the broken dreams and the welfare dependency, the lack of initiative, the people who won't work to improve themselves.

This time there's good news from the mountains; there is local initiative and a bold, workable dream, a chance for Frankfort and Washington to invest in a partnership with a long-neglected community where there's a new, homegrown effort underway.

Gov. Brereton Jones has repeatedly assured us of his concern for eastern Kentucky's social, cultural, and economic welfare. Now it's time for the governor to put his money (and influence) where his mouth is, to encourage full and enthusiastic state and federal support for Elliott County's local initiative.

It's a rare opportunity for the Appalachian Regional Commission to invest in something truly Appalachian, for a change, and for the state tourism and economic development agencies to buy into a workable, overdue local proposal.

Is anybody listening?[20]

More trips resulted in articles on the county for such publications as *Kentucky Living*[21] and this follow-up piece for "Appalachian Voices."

A twelve-hour day in Elliott County could open lots of eyes, particularly for those whose vision of eastern Kentucky is limited to poverty, listlessness, and ignorance.

You won't find any of those traits in the community of folk artists who've made Elliott County the focal point for streams of folklorists, gallery operators, collectors, and curious observers.

Toss your "poor hillbillies" stereotype out the window when you visit Minnie and Garland Adkins in "Peaceful Valley" near Isonville.

Check out the award plaques on Minnie's wall: the 1992 Jane Morton Norton Award for Extraordinary Achievement in the Arts (from Centre College), a Kentucky Arts Council fellowship, the 1994 Annual Award of Distinction from the Folk Art Society of America.

Look at the carvings Minnie is doing to illustrate a new children's book, *Down on the Farm,* with Mike Norris. Don't be surprised by the computer loaded with a drawing program, or by the constant calls and visits from a who's who of museums and folk art collectors.

Maybe what Minnie and Garland Adkins do best, though, is encourage, inspire, and introduce to the market the works of other county folk artists. It's a proud, sharing, supportive attitude that is reflected throughout the community.

Jimmy Lewis was making over twelve dollars an hour working in coal before Minnie convinced him to get serious about his art, and for six years now he has worked full-time carving and painting fish and mermaids or his trademark "Jonah in the belly of the whale."

Tim Lewis served six years in the army and then worked as a logger, miner, trucker, and builder of helicopter wiring harnesses before trying his hand at carving canes in 1988. He moved from walking sticks to sculpting local sandstone a year later, and now you'll find his work in places like the Anton Gallery in Washington, D.C. A certificate for a 1991 Kentucky Arts Council Al Smith Fellowship hangs on the wall of the new house Tim has built by himself on family land; reading material on hand includes *National Geographic* and *Science Digest,* and classical music pours out from the workshop stereo.

Tim Lewis's chisels might uncover a mythical or biblical character in the chunk of sandstone from an old cabin fireplace, or a turtle might emerge from the block. "There's something inside every rock," says Lewis, "if you can find it."

If he could produce them, says Lewis, he could sell fifty sculptures this week. But that wouldn't be any fun. "You create for yourself," says Lewis.

None of Elliott County's artists have had formal training. Leslie Stapleton taught himself to carve and paint detailed, lifelike, and life-size local birds. Junior Lewis used to help his grandpa make hickory bark-bottomed chairs under a rockhouse up the hollow, and he always "fooled around with wood" before getting serious seven years ago. Now his biblical tableaus draw competing collectors, and Junior makes a better living as an artist than he did back when he helped drill oil wells.

You can read about Elliott County's folk artists in a dozen books, in a stream of national magazines, in the glossy gallery and museum catalogs, and in the current newsletter of the North Carolina Folk Art Society. In April you could join Minnie Adkins in Dayton, Ohio, as she shares the podium with art professors and museum curators for a formal presentation on "How the Visual Arts Can Strengthen the Culture."

In June Minnie will be awarded Morehead State University's "Appalachian Treasure" honors, and earlier—May 28–29—Elliott County's artists will host the nation's collectors in Sandy Hook for the second annual Folk Art Festival.

More Kentuckians should make the winding journey to Sandy Hook and Isonville for a close-up look at the Kentucky phenomenon drawing so much national acclaim.

But don't go expecting to find Li'l Abner or Jed Clampett.

Unless, of course, you're willing to fork over a hefty fee to have one of them carved and painted for you.[22]

> Maybe you really can go home again, given sufficient humility and a willingness to learn just how much things have changed. My visits to Elliott County have included lunch with Faye Whitley, visits to folk artists' homes, and a new appreciation for the people and the progress. And I even wrote, for the *Elliott County News,* this attempted explanation.

In October, a very brave local publicity committee asked me to come to Elliott County to help with publicizing the proposed tourism development project tied to the new bridge, community center, and folk art village.

I agreed, and came, but not without a degree of anxiety.

It was but three years ago that my "Home Again" essay in *Appalachian Heritage* set off such an emotional uproar. And, for the current issue of the same journal, I wrote "Gone Too Long," my after the fact reflection on the original essay and on Faye Whitley's even-handed assessment, back then, that I'd been "gone too long" from the mountains.

I agreed, in the second essay, that I wrote the first one in shock, filled with stunned misperceptions, from distorted emotion and four decades of out-of-date memories. I agreed that, yes, I've been gone too long.

So, this time, I came back to Elliott County with both eyes wide open.

I have learned a lot from my two recent trips to Sandy Hook, from meeting many of you, and from reading the two volumes of Elliott County history. And I've learned from driving across the ridge through Gimlet, from revisiting childhood scenes and seeing them now through much older, more perceptive eyes.

I've learned from working with some of the dedicated county leaders who see the new tourism project as a way to create new jobs and new opportunities for young natives who'd like to work at home.

So far I've been met warmly, with an honest, up-front acknowledgment of disagreement with some of my writing—especially the infamous essay—and with good-humored acceptance and frank discussions.

I happen to believe that the bold tourism proposal will work, given adequate cooperation, funding, and time to fully develop. This is not, as David Blair points out, another "pie in the sky" concept. It's workable; it's being developed from within, not handed down from Frankfort or Washington with the usual multiple strings attached.

What little I can do to help, through writing and lobbying, is being done freely and happily. Sort of a small payback, in a sense, for all that Elliott County has given to me during my lifetime.

Family roots, a sense of personal history, and knowing exactly where you come from are—or should be—important to every person of every age. Seeing pictures of my mother, grandfather, and great-grandfather in the Elliott County history strengthened my awareness of my family ties to this land and this way of living; it will always be a part of who I am no matter where I go.

Over the past months I've been making final revisions to a

new book of collected essays, humor columns, and editorials I've published across the region since about 1980. Doing the final editing forced me to take a hard look back at more than a decade of opinionated writing.

At times I laughed at the naive seriousness of my statements; at other times I cringed and wondered if it was really me who'd done such simplistic thinking and writing. I resisted the temptation to rewrite older pieces. The material is, as I explain in the book, what I was thinking when I was writing. People change, continually, and the essays reflect the changes in my own way of looking at the world.

The point, if there is one, is that heritage and progress go hand in hand.

The Elliott County tourism development proposal is a prime example. Natural splendor and local culture are building the future, making use of the past to better the present.[23]

Appalachian Voices

A welcome addition to the *Lexington Herald-Leader* has been a weekly column called "Appalachian Voices," a forum for issues affecting eastern Kentucky, a forum I have used often to say some things I thought needed saying.

The public reaction to my particular "voice" has been predictably mixed.

Some always agree. Some always don't.

Others flip-flop.

Most, probably, don't really give a damn.

But "Appalachian Voices" publication has been a satisfying experience, overall; perhaps it is the best available forum for a point of view that is both "inside" and "outside," both critical and complimentary.

It began, for me, in 1990, with my reaction to the state government's stale old song-and-dance routine that works to put industry into flatter, more prosperous central and northern Kentucky voter centers and advocates the production and sale of handcrafts as the economic salvation for the mountain counties.

After almost thirty years of work in crafts marketing, I felt compelled to write the following column, "Crafts Are Fine, but They're Not a Cure," in response to the ideas being fed to the public by the legislature and state officials.

State economic development efforts in central, northern, or western Kentucky invariably focus on heavy industry. But for the eastern third of the state, Department of Commerce officials offer crafts—the making and selling of quilts, baskets, woodcarvings, and whatever else comes out of the homes and small workshops—as the answer to long-term growth.

Granted, the crafts industry in Kentucky, taken as a whole, is large—maybe accounting for twenty million dollars a year, according to a 1986 survey. But anyone who advocates handcrafts as a major answer has looked neither at history nor reality.

Historically, crafts have provided supplemental income. Berea College's role goes back to 1893, when the Fireside Industries were started as a way for students to earn their education expenses, and today's ubiquitous craft fairs at every crossroads are all descended from Berea's Homespun Fair, first held in 1896 as a way for area crafts producers to sell some work.

Even then, the income was supplemental—income to pay for school, off-season income for small farmers, cash for coverlets woven between everyday farm chores.

Berea College helped organize the missionary movement of the early twentieth century, which preserved the traditional crafts and created the base for current markets. Even that early work was questioned by David Whisnant, whose book *All That Is Native and Fine: The Politics of Culture in an American Region* accused the missionaries of fabricating an artificial Appalachian culture just for the marketplace.

The Southern Highland Handicraft Guild, organized in 1930, was the major factor in the survival of the mountain craft heritage and the creation of today's bustling markets; the guild's Folk Art Center on the Blue Ridge Parkway near Asheville, North Carolina, now includes The Allanstand Shop, a one-million-dollar-a-year retail gallery.

Within the venerable guild, and in Kentucky, the profile of the individual craftsperson has changed dramatically since 1930. There are still the native, self-taught craftspeople, but today's woodworker is more likely to have a fine arts degree. The weavers are fiber artists; the potters are ceramicists, makers of decorative artware. Even the traditional quilts, the ones that sell, are done in contemporary materials and colors.

Skill and design training, market sophistication, and a dedication to craft are factors that cannot be quickly learned or provided by an outside source.

Kentucky is fortunate that state and private efforts have supplemented and continued the early work of Berea College and the Southern Highland Handicraft Guild. The Kentucky Guild of Artists and Craftsmen started in 1961, in partnership at the time with Kentucky's pioneering Department of Commerce crafts marketing effort, and both programs have been widely copied in other states. But some very expensive failures—the Kentucky Design Center, Stanton Woodcraft, etc.—soured the funding agencies' outlook on crafts as economic development.

There are success stories—Appalachian Fireside Crafts (supported by the Save the Children Federation), the Kentucky Department of the Arts Craft Marketing Program, Churchill Weavers, Bybee Pottery, and Berea's series of studio and shop outlets. Overall, the Kentucky craft industry is strong and growing.

But not in Appalachian Kentucky and not in ways that will create long-term jobs and employ large numbers of displaced workers.

The market advantage of handcrafts is their quality, individuality, and limited availability. As the federal government's sixteen-week training programs proved so successfully, the quick fix won't work. The complicated Kentucky Department of Commerce loan program for craftspeople does not work, and capital for equipment and inventory is still a major problem. The market for crafts is out of state; the Berea sales bonanza is fueled by tourists, and more Kentucky crafts are sold in New England than in the commonwealth.

The current public and private craft marketing efforts are good ones, deserving of continued, stronger financial support. The Kentucky Department of Arts broke new ground with its Kentucky Crafts Market, its participation in the New York International Gift Fair, and its valuable referral system. The Kentucky Art and Craft Foundation Gallery in Louisville may just be our finest retail showcase. The Kentucky Guild's Berea fairs still draw crowds after twenty years.

As a statewide industry, crafts are a significant economic factor. But for the lasting economic salvation of eastern Kentucky, look somewhere else. Look to industry, light or heavy, and to the improved schools, water systems, and quality of life necessary to getting those industries to relocate.

The crafts world will continue to grow, to better market its high-quality products, and to better train craftspeople in business operations. But eastern Kentucky needs more than crafts, flea markets, and yard sales to build a lasting, tax-paying economy, and it's time Frankfort realized that.[24]

> I wasn't quite finished with our legislature, though, dominated as it can be by some of our mountain delegates, and in May 1990 I published "Legislature Thinks Flea Markets, Cockfights Enough for Mountains."

To write about Appalachia is often to wind up between a rock and a hard place, caught in an angry crossfire between the natives and the outsiders.

Burned by a hundred years of stereotype and negative publicity, mountaineers are understandably touchy, especially the fairly new middle-class element. With these prosperous mountain residents, the very first mention of poverty, corrupt politics, or poor health care triggers a righteous wrath, an angry denial, a sputtering tirade about new homes, libraries, swimming pools, and high schools.

Outsiders don't like to hear the truth either. That same hundred years of stereotype has the world expecting us all to be bib-overalled, tobacco-chewing, dulcimer-playing, cockfighting, moonshine-drinking, rifle-toting, chair-making, snake-handling, lean-and-lanky hillbillies, quaint ambushers, and sunbonneted granny women in dire need of missionary salvation.

The outsiders don't like to hear the good things about the mountains; the insiders deny the bad.

Eastern Kentucky has, for a hundred years, been the focal point of much of both the good and the bad publicity about the mountaineer. Our music, crafts, feuds, literature, poverty, religions, coal wars, patriotism, educational levels, politics, whiskey, floods, basketball, and humor have been written about, admired, and ridiculed, and splashed across the nation's newspapers and TV screens like no other American region or culture. We've been called hillbillies, briers, mountain folks, happy pappies, and a hundred other catchy labels coined mostly by the media. And, to be honest, there has always been at least a little truth in every one of those labels.

The unpleasant realities that make so many eastern Kentuckians so indignantly angry—high unemployment rates, high dropout and illiteracy rates, a high percentage of substandard housing, and the other statistical negatives—are real, whether we like them or not, and wouldn't go away even if the media focused its glare on more positive issues.

And, though many outsiders don't want to admit it, eastern Kentucky has made giant strides over the past forty years in the development of highways, housing, health care, human services, educational facilities, and—in some areas—economic development.

Remembering how it used to be, thirty and forty years ago, makes the changes appear almost miraculous. Those too young to remember, or new to the area, should read John Day's 1941 book, *Bloody Ground,* reissued in 1981 by the University Press of Kentucky. Day, then a young Lexington reporter, visited snake-handling churches and mountain courtrooms, jenny barns and hillside roadhouses, went on moonshine raids with revenue officers, and wrote about it all from a cynical journalist's viewpoint. It's not a pretty picture of mountain life, but it's mostly accurate, allowing for Day's strong disapproval of the rowdier elements of the mountain lifestyle.

And much of what John Day wrote about, fifty years ago, is still with us, culturally, despite the drastic physical changes.

I am an eastern Kentucky native once removed, and for twenty years have been writing—fact and fiction—about the people and places, the culture and the heritage, that molded all of us into what we are. My fictional characters, like most of us, are flawed and imperfect, modeled on real life. My essays and articles are usually positive, even defensive, but I don't deny reality.

Eastern Kentucky is just as good and just as bad as anyplace else. It is a region judged too harshly by the rest of the world, a region that does have more than its share of problems. Blessed and cursed by coal deposits, rugged terrain, and a fiercely independent culture, the eastern third of Kentucky is a paradox of poverty and plenty, of pride and defeated helplessness.

The problems won't just go away. Educational levels will improve when parents, taxpayers, and teachers *make* them better. Jobs will be created when a better atmosphere for industry exists, when local governments and local residents work together to create the necessary infrastructure and quality of life. Coal won't last forever.

State officials largely ignore the economic needs of eastern Kentucky and take the easy way out, blaming the counties for not doing more to create an industrial environment. But coal severance taxes are not returned to the region to help with that development, and the mythical "Winchester Wall"—the invisible barrier that stops state funds and efforts short—does exist. (For non-Kentuckians, the "Wall" is an imaginary line drawn to separate the eastern third of Kentucky from the more prosperous and better-served Bluegrass region. The city of Winchester sits directly on the line.)

It's a double-edged sword, a damned-if-you-do, damned-if-you-don't standoff, and our legislature spends more time arguing about cockfighting than dealing with real issues. But the general attitude seems to be that cockfighting, flea markets, and crafts are economic stimulus enough for the mountains.

Maybe they're right. Not until we all stop fighting and admit that the War on Poverty isn't over, that all is not well in eastern Kentucky, will anything more get done.

Until then, expect more media coverage similar to the *48 Hours* reports from Floyd and Owsley Counties, more righteous indignation and more useless rhetoric.[25]

> Later, in an entirely different vein but for much the same reasons, I wrote about my grandmother.

When my ninety-eight-year-old grandmother died in May, the women's liberation and feminist rights groups lost a pioneer I'm sure they didn't even know they had.

Grandma must have been what they call a matriarch, the female leader of a sprawling mountain family; she ruled the roost, called the shots, outlived four husbands, and survived life changes that took her from early life in Gimlet in remote Elliott County to her busy final years in urban Ohio. She was never at a loss for words, for courage, for the will to survive that carried her through almost a century of birth, death, tragedy, change, war, a far-flung family, and the tremendous social and physical upheaval as the modern world came to the mountains and then Grandma went boldly out into the world.

Grandma was not a steel magnolia, a slithery southern belle. She was a Kentucky mountain woman, in the rugged mold of Harriette Arnow's fictional Gertie Nevels, a survivor, a no-nonsense woman who could wring a chicken's neck, console a bee-stung grandson, piece a quilt, feed twenty Sunday visitors, and all the while be totally in control.

My years with Grandma were mostly summers and Sundays, in the late 1940s and early 1950s, on a prosperous mountain farm on Elliott County's Mauk Ridge, a lifestyle that was a curious mix of old and new. Sam farmed with a team and a sled, on hillsides too steep for trucks and tractors. The outhouse stood out by the chicken coops, and the water came from a spring-fed well; our heat was from a big fireplace or the cast-iron stove in the kitchen. But then came electricity, in about 1950, then the first television set I ever saw, connected to an antenna a half mile up the ridge. Over the West Virginia channel came the wonder of Pinky Lee, Kate Smith, Howdy Doody, and the never-ending series of boxing matches.

Grandma ruled with an iron fist tempered by genuine love and concern. She sent me every day to the post office and store, just over the ridge, and always there was a nickel extra for candy. When the family chipped in to buy Grandma a new electric range, she swore me to secrecy: during the week she cooked on the old iron stove, but on Sunday morning she'd try again to use the fancy new appliance so nobody's feelings would get hurt.

Grandma was an equal partner, or more, in life on Mauk Ridge. Her iron-willed presence was always felt in any and all decisions. Her husband, my step-grandfather Sam, was a progressive man who valued education. Though we were no blood kin, Sam Leedy was my closest friend and model, the man who helped raise me when my father went to the war, the man whose gentle, patient presence is always with me.

The War—World War II—touched Grandma's family hard. One young uncle spent over a year in a German prison camp; Daddy was on an LST (landing ship, tank) in the English Channel; and

I'm sure one of Grandma's dying thoughts was about my uncle Paul, a navy pilot who survived the war only to be lost when his bomber vanished on a routine mission.

I grew away from Grandma—we had our own tobacco to raise, then there was baseball, school, and girls—and then I endorsed Grandma's high school graduation check for ten dollars over at Berea College as my admission deposit. When Sam died, Grandma moved to Ohio. I moved to North Carolina, so for over twenty years my news came second and thirdhand. Grandma cut off her hair, remarried, traveled, made and sold quilts, buried another husband, kept on going on.

The last time I saw Grandma was in about 1982. She was visiting in Olive Hill, I was on my way to a meeting in West Virginia, so I stopped off to see if Grandma would still remember me. She did. "The little black shiny-eyed feller," she smiled. Grandma was about ninety then, working on her quilts, and still looking, to me, exactly as she had thirty years earlier.

When my mother called to tell me Grandma was dying, my response was simply to say "Well, that just means she's decided it's time." Grandma would, I was certain, choose death on her terms; she would die as she had lived, with courage and self-determination.

I do not grieve over Grandma's death.

She lived almost a century, saw the dramatic progress that came suddenly to the Kentucky mountains, saw her own children, grandchildren, great-grandchildren, and even her great-great-grandchildren make their own ways in the world; she lived a full life and died proudly.

But Grandma will live forever in her descendants, the stubborn and self-sufficient women and men who may not even ever know where their strength comes from but who'll always be a little different because Grandma did things her way back before the women's movement had ever been invented.[26]

> My warm memories of the mountains turned a little ugly later that same year, when my son and my youngest brother went to Saudi Arabia with the 101st Airborne to help provide the manpower for George Bush's only grand moment.

> Written for "Appalachian Voices," my essay "Willingness to Fight for America Is Being Whittled Down, Even in Patriotic Appalachia" ran instead as an editorial, a bitter expression of how I came to view the patriotic support mountaineers usually offer to whatever the government wants.

In the honored old mountain way, my son and youngest brother have gone off to war. They're in Saudi Arabia with the proud 101st Airborne, defending our right to cheap oil.

When my grandfather fought the "War to End All Wars," the cause was more noble. My granddaddy Cox's answer, when asked why he had volunteered to fight in World War I, was "So that my sons won't have to fight."

On December 7, 1941, my grandfather's reasoning fell victim to the world economy, blind aggression, and Japanese warplanes. My father and my uncles were off to the South Pacific, to Italy, France, and Germany; off to fight the last "good war." Troops in World War II knew exactly who the enemy was, and why we had to win.

Then, when my father finally did get to come home, he met me, two years old, trying stubbornly to run him, this strange man, out of my mother's house.

We were all the wrong age for the Korean "police action," but during the Vietnam era two brothers and two brothers-in-law served, supporting the only war ever fought by body count—the daily scorecard. This political disaster cost us fifty-eight thousand young American lives.

If anything good came out of Vietnam, it was the abolition of the local draft boards, the small, smug groups that used the draft as a way to protect the well-to-do and rid their communities of the rowdy, lower-income young men whose parents didn't have enough clout.

Even in patriotic Appalachia, Vietnam wore down the fighting zeal. It cost our government the unflagging support and willingness to serve that have been the mountain way since Kentuckians marched to New Orleans in 1814 to repel the British invasion.

But now, we're sending our sons off to war again. This time it's different in that most are volunteers in the "new" army; they are well conditioned, well equipped, well trained, and generally a little older than the teen-age soldiers who were shipped to Vietnam.

In Saudi Arabia, my son Greg surely won't have to stand guard with an unloaded M-16, the standard practice in most duty stations. But even the live ammo, tents under desert sun, nerve gas, the PLO, and the next-door presence of an Arab Hitler can't get him combat pay. By army definition, Saudi Arabia is not a combat zone. Yet.

So, there'll be no combat pay until somebody gets shot.

Casual military estimates of potential United States casualties, the debate as to just how much loss is "acceptable," and George Bush's politically motivated macho stance do little to console the families, spouses, and children of the U.S. soldiers in Saudi Arabia. To me, cheap oil and a second term for George Bush aren't worth even one American life.

My son and my brother will do their duty, do what they've been trained to do. They are professional soldiers, good ones, award-winning performers. They, and all the troops, deserve our full support, our concern, our prayers.

But I'd rather they were doing what they're supposed to do—defend our country—instead of being used as political pawns in a two-thousand-year-old struggle that probably will never end.[27]

> Once the real fighting started in Desert Storm, I became outspoken hawk: I could not, in my heart, separate the protests against the war from protests against my son being a soldier, and I became a vocal opponent of those who would criticize our troops.
>
> For, as I explained often, back then, I only have one son. And they're trying to get him killed. I wrote, for the East Tennessee State University publication *Now and Then,* my confused poem, "Video Game."

I can't sleep any more
And it's just as well.

All the better to watch CNN

The war, live and in color,
Around the clock.

SCUDs, Tomahawks, Patriots,
Other volatile "assets"
Rain in both directions.

        The sky is falling.

Laser-guided smart bombs,
Shells the size of cars.

It's hard to tell, on TV,
Just whose missiles and mortars

        Are whose.

It's a scorecard war;
Get your program, popcorn
And cold beer.

It's a hell of a war.
And a good thing war is so awful

        The famous general said,
Lest we should grow
Too fond of it.

And he didn't even have TV
Back then, on Virginia hillsides.

        Just box seats and binoculars

At the home field,
With a picnic lunch.

Maybe baseball wasn't
the only entertainment
        We invented

During the Civil War.[28]

After the Desert Storm debacle, I almost caused another small war, closer to home. I wrote "Kentucky Dialect Could Give You a Certain Advantage; Bad Grammar Could Kill It" for "Appalachian Voices" after much thinking about why our

> Berea College graduates sometimes lost out in final job interviews.

Most of us eastern Kentuckians—maybe most rural Kentuckians—have to learn a second language when we go out into the world.

English.

The kind they speak in businesses, in offices, on television, during job interviews, in classrooms.

I'm not talking accents—a Kentucky drawl actually can be an effective tool, used in the right places—I mean grammar, pronunciation, and enunciation, the basic English language as spoken in most of the United States.

Nobody loves the Kentucky dialect, the colorful wordage, and the twangy cadences better than I do, but in most of the world our native speech earns us labels we don't want. Labels like "hillbilly," "redneck," "hick."

However they're spelled, those labels used in contempt all mean "inferior."

That's totally unfair. Always has been, always will be. But that's the way it is. Blacks and Hispanics deal with the exact same problem; our native speech patterns get doors slammed in our faces, limit our ability to communicate, get us branded as culturally and intellectually deficient.

Everybody in the world speaks at several different levels. There is formal language, casual language, jargon, slang, and regional dialect. Every level of language has its place, its uses, its labels.

Learning what to do when is the crucial concept.

Working on a college campus, I'm exposed every day to a specialized speech that I try very hard to understand but often have to have interpreted: the "inside" language of young people is a foreign language to any of us over thirty. What some students forget, or never learn, is that the world after graduation speaks a simpler, more universal, more understandable language.

Corporate job interviewers freeze at the sound of slang or a regional dialect. So do other interviewers, business leaders, editors, and educators; only in the world of politics does an exaggerated accent and folksy down-home dialect seem to be helpful, and those who use that ploy surely practice before they preach.

Many years ago I resented and resisted Berea College's efforts to teach me how to talk, how to eat at a formal dinner, how to dress for success. But I did listen, watch, and learn. I clung to my roots, my dialect, my distinctive culture, but I also learned how to play the game. And to speak everyday English.

As a story teller, fiction writer, and humorist, I make heavy use of eastern Kentucky language patterns. I slip casually in and out of the different layers of the English language, but don't consider any one layer to be superior to another. The rules have relaxed; there's no longer "the" proper grammar. What's right depends totally upon who and where you are.

But the fact remains. To avoid unfair labeling, to get a toe in the door, even we rustics need to learn mainstream English. If this is an unpleasant compromise, so be it.

The choice is pretty clear.[29]

> That particular essay, which provoked answering "Appalachian Voices" that accused me of selling out, probably marked a small beginning, a subtle shift of direction, maybe a weariness with the stubborn pride that so often costs us so much in eastern Kentucky.
>
> But I simply couldn't resist, when wealthy horseman and native West Virginian Brereton Jones was elected governor, wading back into the fray. Perhaps my history of mixed love and conflict with my family's home county helped create the opinion that the *Herald-Leader* titled "Just Look . . . Jones Can See Real Money Woes in Elliott."

It probably would be too much to expect that a governor who can afford to lend himself a million dollars to get elected could really relate to an unemployment rate of 23 percent in Elliott County.

He may not even know there *is* an Elliott County. Or that there is unemployment.

But official statistics are based only on those who apply for unemployment benefits during a four-week period, and the University of Kentucky's Appalachian Center estimates the *real* unemployment rate in Elliott County at over 60 percent.

That's six out of ten. Six out of a hundred is the national rate.

During last spring's East Kentucky Leadership Conference in

Pikeville, Al Smith recalled how the late Harry Caudill often wondered if maybe a relocation service would be the best service to offer the area's young people.

I'm sure Caudill was aware that an effective relocation service has been in operation for at least fifty years, a true home industry that gradually relocated relatives north to Ohio. It's one of the few things we could do without government restrictions, so I'm sort of grateful Caudill never made a formal proposal and attracted the bureaucrats.

Caudill, whose books and actions were a major reason the Appalachian Regional Commission was created, had to watch that agency ignore the rural areas it was intended to assist, to watch ARC strangle itself in red tape, politics, and unfinished efforts.

Caudill's death, and that of Gov. Bert Combs, cost eastern Kentucky its two most powerful voices. Whether or not you agreed with either man—and nobody ever did, totally—they both were listened to in powerful circles. Both fought for eastern Kentucky. Both recognized the region's strengths and weaknesses. Both earned accolades and anger from the population.

For more than three decades, two powerful men fought the good fight; but far too often they fought it alone.

When, twenty years from now, the coal is finally gone, Caudill's relocation service may *have* to be implemented.

It was done once before, when the North Carolina Cherokees were dispatched along the Trail of Tears to Oklahoma. That was for different reasons—white men *wanted* the Indian land—and the only people other than the residents who want most of eastern Kentucky are the landfill operators.

There are still those who want the coal and timber, what's left, but they're the same corporate entities that have been bleeding the region for two hundred years.

Frankfort gives lip service to eastern Kentucky's economic problems. And, surely, when he moved here from West Virginia, Governor Jones at least drove across the northeast spur of the state.

On his next trip back home the governor should leave I-64 at Morehead and cruise up U.S. 32 into Elliott County and visit the land-locked pocket the state would rather didn't exist. The governor won't find any bankrupt horse farms, any millionaires needing a government bailout, or any Japanese factories in Elliott County; he'll find survivors, fighters, workers, people who've found ways to cling to their land and lifestyles and who—with a little recognition and help from the governor—could start to revitalize the economy and put 60 percent of the population back to work.

He'll find a stubbornly proud people, a willing and competent work force that lacks only opportunity.

Campaign financing is not Kentucky's major current problem. A 23 percent unemployment rate, anywhere, is a disgrace. A 60 percent unemployment rate is inhumane.[30]

The emotional essay brought a rare and welcome positive result: a letter from Ann Caudill, the widow of the late Harry Caudill. "I cannot tell you how touched and pleased I am," she wrote, "that you have remembered Harry and his constant effort to find solutions, and to awaken the effective interest of the people. It was, indeed, as you said, mostly a lonely fight, but he was always encouraged, as I am, by people like you who listened and took action. Thank you for continuing the battle for recognition of the plight of the eastern counties with your article.

"Your piece surely deserves comment, and from the governor, action."[31]

From the governor, I *got* action. The Monday after the column ran in the Sunday edition, Governor Jones called to both protest and promise. He *did* know eastern Kentucky, Jones protested. He *would* do something, the governor promised.

And do it now.

A polished politician, calling from the state's most powerful position, can easily overwhelm a wide-eyed comparative innocent unfamiliar with the persuasive ability of a pro.

I believed Governor Jones.

I think *he* believed, early in his administration, his promises of a decisive move to straighten twisty U.S. high-

> way 32 into Sandy Hook and to establish some new industry in Elliott County. He *did* begin the process by meeting with the county's legislators.
>
> But budgets, scandals, and FBI investigations sort of distracted everybody in Frankfort, and I relearned a necessary lesson: don't believe anything a governor promises until *after* it's actually done.
>
> Especially if you are not a major campaign contributor.
>
> As mentioned earlier, the "Appalachian Voices" column sometimes creates a continuing dialogue, as it did when I later responded to Ron Daly's essay asking for "transplanted" eastern Kentuckians to speak out in support of their homeland.
>
> There *are* lots of former mountaineers in powerful places outside the region. Most *don't* openly support legislation, economic development programs, or anything else directed toward the mountain counties.
>
> And, so, I wrote again.

Regarding Ron Daly's recent plea for transplanted eastern Kentuckians to speak up for their homeland, there's more to the issue than meets the eye.

Some of us *do* speak up, but sometimes we don't say exactly what the "Hindman Mafia"—the small but influential group of leaders and politicians centered around Hindman—wants to hear.

We *are* concerned, we care, and there's an almost blind loyalty to the land and people we love so much.

Almost.

Some of us argue that eastern Kentucky must face and deal with some internal problems at the same time it receives added recognition, appreciation, and political clout.

Constructive criticism is seldom welcome anywhere, and eastern Kentucky is no exception. That's stating the case mildly.

The right questions are often more important than the right answers, in terms of progress, and when the questions are stifled so is the development. A problem cannot be solved until it is identified. And, even then, the issue may not be one that can be easily resolved, but may instead lead to further questions that will shed more light on the situation.

A pat answer is almost always wrong, almost always an admission of defeat or of a job half done.

I happen to strongly agree with Ron Daly that transplanted eastern Kentuckians could—and should—take a much more active role. We *can* communicate to our elected representatives that a century or so of neglect is more than enough, that *all* the coal severance tax should go back to the producing counties, that state economic development efforts shouldn't stop at the Winchester Wall.

Some transplanted eastern Kentuckians are in powerful positions, and they could use their influence to funnel more business and more concern toward the mountains.

Most don't.

And I wish I knew why.

Some, I assume, are simply ashamed to let anybody know where they're from. A lifetime of being treated as an inferior because of a mountain accent and cultural background can do strange things to a person; to get ahead, to be socially accepted, many former eastern Kentuckians have erased all traces of their upbringing.

And, worse, some have adopted the elitist disdain for mountain ways and accepted the view that nothing will ever change in eastern Kentucky anyhow.

A two-sided effort is needed.

Mountain leaders must convince the former residents that the old politics have given way to a new era of progressive planning and service, that quality education is a priority, that cockfighting legislation is presented tongue-in-cheek.

If that is really the case.

The transplants must realize that they're in a position to be of direct help, that their heritage is one to display with pride, not shame, and that modern political decisions are based on noise and numbers.

I am a transplant, to the edge of the Bluegrass, thirty years removed from everyday life in eastern Kentucky.

But I still care, deeply and passionately, and I'm as stubbornly committed to speaking out—either direction—as anyone could be.

Where are the rest of you?[32]

> Daly and other eastern Kentucky leaders soon rallied to the support of Chris Perkins, the outgoing U.S. representative from the mountain district, a defense I considered to be a blind attack on anyone who would criticize the politics of the mountains. At the same time, a handful of eastern Kentucky leaders argued that the more prosperous mountain areas—Ashland, London, etc.—should no longer be considered part of Appalachia. I responded, as always.

Some of eastern Kentucky's political leaders seem to have learned about media coverage from the University of Kentucky basketball program: any in-depth analysis or critical comment is taken as a personal affront, almost as treason, and only glowing success stories should be printed or aired.

But, for all its rigged testing, thousand-dollar shipments, NCAA probations, and its dandified coach whose annual gross income exceeds that of some entire mountain counties, UK's basketball program looks clean as a whistle compared to Chris Perkins.

Carl Perkins is rightly revered by eastern Kentucky. He was a leader, a doer, an advocate for the mountains, a political figure of stature equal to Bert Combs and John Sherman Cooper.

His son inherited the last name and the seat in the U.S. Congress and shamed them both. He has, if anything, been treated gently by the media, out of respect for his father's legend, but that would have ended had not the younger Perkins withdrawn from the current race.

I happen to agree with the media bashing of Paul Patton's vote to kill the seatbelt bill. Whether Patton actually voted his conscience or voted to pacify the political pressures, I'd wager that his vote was cast with more concern for the next gubernatorial race than for basic human freedoms.

It would have been a weak decision no matter where Patton was from; the fact that he's from Pikeville caused part of the blame to be laid on traditional eastern Kentucky politics as usual.

The angry defensiveness of much of Appalachian Kentucky surely stems from two centuries of hillbilly stereotype, but a stubborn refusal to deal with reality simply confirms some of the outsider concepts.

Mountain leaders can't simply bury their heads in the strip mines and ignore the statistical and human realities of unemployment, population loss, corruption in county and school administration, and the lack of a stable economic base. The media does not *make* the news; it just reports it.

It seems eastern Kentucky is now being redefined, shrunk down to Knott, Floyd, Pike, and Perry Counties, the larger coalfields destined to suffer when, in twenty years or less, the mining stops.

Being a once-removed eastern Kentuckian who does not pay homage to anybody named Perkins, Stumbo, or Patton, who still considers Ashland and London to be part of the region, I realize that—according to some mountain leaders—I am not entitled to any opinion except to voice unflagging support for the way things are.

Those of us who've left the mountains—by choice or by circumstance—are sometimes in an even better position to effectively and objectively evaluate our homeland. We're not *supposed* to evaluate, according to many, and whenever we dare point out a problem we're labeled "traitor" or dismissed with a "he's been gone from the mountains too long" shrug of annoyance.

Blind loyalty is better suited to UK basketball than to a region's destiny.

But UK's turnaround on the hardwood could also serve as an example to eastern Kentucky's political powers. It's better to recognize the problems, deal with them, and look forward, not backwards.

And, maybe, also by UK example, some new faces and new forces could speed up the process.[33]

> When another "Voices" writer suggested that eastern Kentucky was missing the boat by not capitalizing more on the tourism industry, my response was, of course, to write "First Things First."

Tourism surely is, as Clyde Pack wrote in "Appalachian Voices" (May 16), a potential eastern Kentucky growth industry that has barely been tapped, a flow of outside income we'd do well to actively court and to count on as a lasting resource.

There are, however, a few drawbacks.

Tourism, as a recent study of Sevier County, Tennessee (home of Gatlinburg and Dollywood), indicated, creates primarily seasonal, minimum-wage employment, low-level service jobs. The dollar impact is deceptive, spread broadly across the economy, difficult to properly measure and evaluate.

There is even a cultural impact, not always a positive change: a "them and us" mentality can develop, a simmering hostility toward the outsiders, or a weary acceptance of the long lines, delays, rudeness, and different ways that can create an even larger gulf between natives and tourists.

But tourism *is* a clean source of new dollars, an industry that does not deplete natural resources, a source of steady income that is, probably, the fastest growing of all industries nationwide.

So why doesn't eastern Kentucky, given its natural bounty, reap a larger share?

The lame old excuse was bad roads, bad services (restaurants and lodging), and a rough-and-ready local lifestyle hostile to "outsiders."

Now we have roads. Restaurants aplenty, in most areas, plus hospitals, shopping centers, lakes, and state parks.

But we also have pollution, clattering coal trucks, a glaring lack of cooperative development and promotion, and—worst of all—the lingering image of a shoot-first-ask-questions-later mentality backed up by ongoing media coverage.

Before anybody builds a gigantic theme park (Rooster World?), opens more music barns, or brings in the outlet malls, we'd do well to first clean up the image. Clean up the creekbeds and roadways. Haul off the old engine blocks, school bus bodies, refrigerator shells, and abandoned coal-mining machines.

Drive down and take a clear-eyed look at the heavily visited mountains of east Tennessee, western North Carolina, and north Georgia. You'll find clean, uncluttered roadways and waterways, controls on industrial development at the expense of natural beauty, and a concern for preservation mixed in with all the glitter and gaudy gadgets.

Dig a little deeper and you'll find a long history of cooperative development and advertising, a willingness to set personal differences aside and work to recruit the tourism dollars. You'll find a hefty tax on rooms and meals, a nifty system designed to make tourists pay for the advertising that helped them decide to visit.

Tourism *is* a business. It requires investment, management, marketing, and a major commitment, top to bottom.

For eastern Kentucky, the hardest obstacle to overcome—to open the doors to increased tourism—is the national image of grinding poverty, feuds, crooked politics, and desolation caused by strip mining.

That's a tough test, a marketing and management task unlike any other, a long-term project that may not be doable.

But there won't be an influx of tourism into the mountains until travelers feel comfortable and know there's something rewarding to see and do. They won't come until they know it's safe. We all know that's a pretty absurd way to look at an entire region, but tourists don't.

So there's work to do before travel becomes a major industry in the Kentucky mountains. Dollywood isn't the answer, just yet.[34]

> In July 1993, I wrote again about my native Elliott County, depressed once again by unemployment reports, a column entitled "You Won't Hear Applause for Elliott's No. 1 Rating."

Elliott County is number one again.

For the sixteenth consecutive month, with an official jobless rate of 24.7 percent, this tiny pocket of otherwise forgotten northeast Kentucky leads the list.

Some nearby neighbors also made the top ten: unemployment is rampant in Magoffin (20 percent), Carter (15.8 percent), and Lewis (14.4 percent), all almost within hollering distance of Sandy Hook. In Morgan County the rate is 13.9 percent, and relatively prosperous Pike County reported the same level.

Statewide, unemployment stands at 7.1 percent.

And, to quote the news report, "The rates do not reflect people who have not actively looked for work in four weeks."

So it's safe, in most counties, to double the official unemployment rate to get the actual, real, depressing numbers.

That would put Elliott at 49.4 percent; Magoffin up to 40

percent; Carter to 31.6 percent, despite the reported annual state subsidy to the Carter Caves State Park of $448,395.

The governor is, of course, too busy dealing with the $200–300 million overall state budget shortfall to be bothered with such mere trifles as half of Elliott County's work force standing idle. The governor will, he says, "trim the fat" to balance the budget, but so far about the only announced cuts have been to education.

Which is probably sort of okay, according to the *Herald-Leader*'s Bill Bishop, who reports that education levels in rural Kentucky don't seem to affect the economy anyhow, that the real problem is a deficit of good jobs, not good workers. That's true, but it's a little like arguing about which came first, the chicken or the egg.

Well-educated eastern Kentuckians do migrate outward, in force, to find adequate employment. Official economic development efforts for the eastern third of Kentucky are all geared toward the five-dollar-per-hour, low-end, low-skill jobs.

When a cheap, plentiful labor pool is offered as the major inducement to locate a factory, the inevitable result is the presence of old-fashioned sweatshop operations, cut-and-sew variations aimed primarily at female workers.

Rather than commute fifty to a hundred miles per day on bad roads, for minimum wage, most workers will choose welfare.

That's not laziness, sorriness, or lack of moral fiber.

That's plain and simple arithmetic.

Not working pays better than working at the level of jobs the state promotes for eastern Kentucky.

If decent jobs were available, the more-educated natives would stay at home. If jobs requiring higher skill levels were offered, those higher levels would be acquired.

I doubt that anybody in Elliott County is proud of their number one ranking. Good people live in the land Frankfort has forgotten.

The last time I wrote about this very same issue, the new governor called with passionate promises of immediate action.

I suspect that by now he's learned better than to make specific promises he can't keep.[35]

> A month later, again responding to a *Herald-Leader* editorial, I wrote "Politics Make ARC Worthless to Eastern Kentucky."

As Bill Bishop pointed out last week, President Clinton is "wasting his chance to fix ARC's woes."

The Appalachian Regional Commission (ARC) is due a new leader, a political appointment to replace George Bush's lame duck federal director.

According to Bishop, Clinton has two choices: a West Virginian handpicked by West Virginia Democrat Robert Byrd (to continue that state's 33 percent slice of the ARC budget pie) or Clinton's "old buddy," Jessie White, allegedly the more qualified of the two candidates.

Actually, Clinton has a third, more logical, option.

He could lop two hundred million dollars a year from the federal deficit by abolishing an agency far too hamstrung by politics to justify its further existence.

About the only places ARC would be visibly missed are West Virginia and Alabama, recipients of over half the agency's current funding (54 percent vs. Kentucky's 7 percent).

Even the late Harry Caudill, whose 1960s writings and activism helped create the ARC—as, Caudill envisioned, an intensive federal effort based on the Tennessee Valley Authority—grew disillusioned with the waste and politics that watered a noble concept down into a private slush fund for the region's senators and governors.

Of course, every U.S. president since Lyndon B. Johnson has attempted a shutdown of ARC, but has been thwarted by the power of Sen. Robert Byrd, that renowned West Virginia fiddle player and grand master of pork barrel politics who will, if he lives long enough, surely relocate most of the federal bureaucracy from D.C. to the urban eastern areas of the Mountain State.

I do agree with Bill Bishop that if ARC is to ever function effectively it must redefine its territory. Eliminate mountainous Mississippi, the peaks of Alabama, and the remote wilderness of New York. Concentrate on the southwestern coalfields of

West Virginia and on eastern Kentucky and better define eligibility even in those pockets.

The ARC version of Appalachian Kentucky is generous to a fault. Prosperous, rolling Madison County is not much more "Appalachian" than is downtown Louisville, except for the presence of Berea College and its almost 150 years of service to the mountains. The south-central counties now included as part of ARC's service area may very well need the services (if, indeed, any such services actually existed), but those counties are by no means "Appalachian."

Bill Clinton is wasting an opportunity. Unfortunately, that seems to be the president's working pattern: it should already be obvious even to Clinton that he has but one term in which to make his mark, and at the rate he's proceeding it'll take Clinton three more years just to fill all the open positions (such as the ARC director's slot).

Senator Byrd does not work so inefficiently or slowly.

Or so ineffectively.

So we can expect to see, should Clinton ever actually get around to making the appointment, West Virginia's Mike Wenger appointed to head the Appalachian Regional Commission.

Expect to see West Virginia's share go up to 75 percent.

And expect to see eastern Kentucky continue to be ignored by the very agency that was created because of the needs and leadership of eastern Kentucky.

The only valid solution I see, the only way to get ARC efforts and funds where they're needed, is to convince Robert Byrd to move to Hindman or Hazard.[36]

> A belated reading of Henry Shapiro's *Appalachia on Our Mind* produced this "Appalachian Voices" essay on "otherness":

Henry D. Shapiro, in his book *Appalachia on Our Mind,* referred to the Appalachian "otherness" that has kept a people and a culture set apart from the rest of the United States for most of a century.

Lots of the "otherness" was—and still is—a clever marketing concept fostered by turn-of-the-century missionaries. It was a way to sell mountain crafts, music, and dance to a nation eager to believe such pure Anglo-Saxon stock still existed.

There was a touch of a racist attitude in daily practice at the time, which assumed that all mountaineers had the cultural and psychological capacity to participate in the usage of their culture and therefore ought to be taught to practice what we'd forgotten.

Agencies and "folk schools" worked to teach mountain folk their own culture, to make us back into "song-singers and tale-tellers, shingle-makers and weavers, dyers and basket-makers."

We were perceived, early in this century, as an isolated, lily-white, undiluted, and uncorrupted (by worldly influences) pocket of quaint and desirable "otherness."

The Appalachian "other" has grown into a robust contemporary marketplace for mountain crafts, story telling, and music, although today's practitioners are more likely to be college-trained imports who share none of the region's real heritage or bloodlines.

There *is* an Appalachian "otherness" alive and well today.

A stubborn, dry-humored, almost rednecked "other," a refusal to be homogenized into the mainstream America, a culture of pickup trucks, country music, and an almost perverse pride at having survived the many noble efforts to properly civilize such a rowdy population.

Lots of us "others" have adopted a protective veneer, a surface acceptability, a sheen of sophistication necessary for employment and social interaction. But dig deep enough, gouge hard enough, trigger the stubborn "otherness," and you'll get a taste of the real old-fashioned mountaineer.

A taste you may not like. A taste of the personality that caused the missionary workers to work so hard and so in vain to ban the evil banjo and moonshine from the effort to help us become ourselves.

Let's all give thanks that they did not succeed. And give praise to the Appalachian "otherness."[37]

> When surveys showed that eastern Kentucky physicians prescribe tranquilizers in massive quantities, I responded with "Nerve Pills a Symptom of Neglect of the Region."

The "nerve pill nirvana" flap in eastern Kentucky points out just how much progress we've made over the past forty years.

There was a time when tranquilizers were the opiate of just the rich and famous, the urban wealthy whose physicians readily supplied whatever was most socially in demand. Legal and illegal drugs have always been available to the elite, with hardly a chirp from the watchful media.

Now that there's Valium for the masses, it's a social disease.

Now that nerve pills are supplied to eastern Kentuckians, it's further evidence of genetic defects, political corruption, and all the other stereotypical conclusions so automatically drawn whenever mountain people are part of any issue.

The heavy nerve pill usage in eastern Kentucky is a symptom, not a disease.

Lump the nerve pills in with the drinking, killing, and depression of a region and a culture that has been being slowly bled to death for 150 years, that has been slowly robbed of its natural resources, its young people, and its pride; a culture that has been ridiculed for its traditions, its religion, and its folkways and has been discussed, dissected, and discarded by experts who'd never dare set foot east of Winchester.

Look at the unemployment rates, the per capita income levels, the percentage of people who live below federal poverty levels.

Look inside the souls of people who've struggled just to survive, who've endured a lifetime of hard work and loss, who've watched their children be forced to move away, who've lived without the modern medical care and human services so taken for granted in urban America.

Look to the near future, to the time when the coal and timber are all gone, to a time when all the decades of government neglect can no longer be offset by selling away the resources.

You'll need nerve pills, too, when you absorb the bleak reality.

Physicians everywhere are perhaps too ready to prescribe nerve pills, and those doctors in the mountains are no exception.

Back in the late 1940s, when I rebelled at having to go back to the same room of the old Goddard School in Fleming County (I'd already *had* that room, the one for the first and second grades, the way I saw it), the doctor prescribed little green "nerve pills" to help cure my sudden blindness.

Fortunately, I couldn't swallow pills.

My dog Pal took more of them than I did, but I stayed at home for half a school year.

My eyesight dramatically returned just in time for the start of third grade in another room.

I suspect today's nerve pill users would experience a similar miraculous recovery if conditions were to suddenly improve the way they did for me way back then.

But that's unlikely, maybe even impossible, in eastern Kentucky.

It's hard to undo two centuries of neglect and economic abuse overnight.

Don't blame the situation on the nerve pills, though.

They're just treating a symptom of a two-hundred-year-old disease.[38]

> An anonymous respondent didn't agree with anything I had to say about "nerve pills." This person wrote, on an unsigned postcard:
>
> > Au contraire, Mssr. Perfessor
> >
> > The flow of traffic toward Moonshine, Meprobamate [a prescription tranquilizer, I finally learned], and Misappropriated School Monies is a strong indicator of "Mountaineer" mentality.
> >
> > Rather than fight against the tide of neglect, abuse, and hardship, most of these "rugged individualists" would rather embrace a psychedelic escape—trip and lie there, fondling it, in the warm muck.
> >
> > These people are low and adamantly *hold themselves* lower than any government or society ever could. The spirit is corrupted from within, and *not* impeded from without.[39]
>
> I don't get to spend much time "fondling it in the warm muck" these days, busy as I stay adamantly holding myself low.
>
> The unsigned message does, I'm afraid, accurately represent the opinion many central Kentuckians (and even some transplanted mountaineers) hold of eastern Kentucky. In fairness, even *I* sometimes would like to light a fire un-

> der those who so easily give in to outside influence, who surrender without even a struggle, who simply blame it all on someone else and give up.
>
> But blanket condemnations—especially from critics unwilling to sign their missives—are no more valid here than they are anywhere else. I include the preceding sample simply as evidence of the level of response my writing can generate.
>
> I do not bury my head in the "warm muck" and ignore basic problems as I see them; I question both "inside" and "outside" influences that shape a region's future.
>
> I *can* be a cheerleader, especially when I see local forces organize and embrace a dream. The willingness to make the effort, to make big plans, is more important than the eventual success or failure of a single project.
>
> I applaud every sign of native voices speaking out, of local initiative helping shape the future.
>
> We need more local voices, more native leadership, more evidence of people taking charge of their own lives.
>
> Mine is perhaps a weary "Appalachian" voice, a voice wondering if any of it really does any good, a voice often disillusioned by the endless process.
>
> Much of my disenchantment with government (at all levels) now gets expressed in my sometimes barbed "Head of the Holler" humor column, but I couldn't resist responding when newspaper reports of the 1994 East Kentucky Leadership Conference seemed to indicate more concern about image than about concrete action.

Another University of Kentucky study has discovered—for the nth time—that Appalachian Kentucky trails the rest of the state and all of the nation in economic activity and per capita income levels.

Harry Caudill told us that, and told us why, over thirty years ago.

UK's Appalachian Center report, "Kentucky's Distressed Communities," is a much-needed continuation, or, as the *Herald-Leader* editorial page put it, "a call to action."

Others have called before, though, angrily and often, with very little resulting response.

Now, some mountain leaders have suggested another kind of call.

"1-800-HILLBILLY."

The tongue-in-cheek suggestion by *Louisville Courier-Journal* editor David Hawpe would create a toll-free line for reporting negative news media references to eastern Kentucky's "hillbillies."

Since the Kentucky legislature recently attempted to establish a state agency to censor the news, Hawpe's 800-line suggestion wasn't so far-fetched.

According to the Associated Press report, Appalshop's Herb E. Smith *did* point out, during the East Kentucky Leadership Conference, that there's a fine line between the region's image and its reality. Fix what's wrong, he seemed to suggest, and the image will correct itself.

Rather than indignantly foaming at the mouth over the "hillbilly" image, eastern Kentucky's leaders would do better to address the ten counties with a poverty rate of 42 percent and deal with the likelihood that the Appalachian Regional Commission won't ever alter its political funding method of investing in "growth areas" while ignoring the "pockets of extreme distress."

All the experts have already told us that the answer to Appalachian economic woes is sustained local development, but none of them have told us just how to accomplish that. Jobs in the service industries are the prevailing national growth pattern, but services are contingent upon an employed population that can afford to make use of those services.

Without a solid economic base—such as that once provided by coal—service providers don't have any customers (except the state, federal, and county agencies). Some of these agencies are suffering, too, because property taxes don't get collected (because there are no jobs to earn the money to pay the taxes?).

Actually, if the uncollected tax statistics follow the pattern established by the recent undervalued property scandals, it'll turn out to be the more affluent citizens who aren't paying up.

All of which leads me to suggest that the contemporary negative "hillbilly" image rides more with the corruption of elected officials and the blatant abuses of the people and the land by some business leaders.

We ordinary hillbillies just get attention for cockfighting, hound dogs, pickup trucks, country music, and corn pone.

Positive media attention can't be forced.

It *can* be earned.

Maybe the beleaguered east Kentucky leaders can take some small comfort in Bill Bishop's attention to Rick Pitino's soap opera style of manipulating fan emotions: if Bishop stays busy with such earthshaking issues, maybe the pattern of sweatshop economic development in the eastern Kentucky won't surface for a week or two.

Call 1-800-HILLBILLY to express your opinions.[40]

> Finally, when the United States Census Bureau reported that seven of the top twenty-five U.S. poorest counties were in Kentucky, I wrote about our lofty rankings and the "pockets" of poverty that distort the perceptions:

Seven Kentucky counties made the national top twenty-five.

According to the U.S. Census Bureau's 1990 County and City Data Book, as reported in the September 6 *Herald–Leader,* the top twenty-five poorest counties list includes McCreary (number 7), Elliott (number 8), Edmundson (number 10), Menifee (number 15), Jackson (number 17), Owsley (number 19), and Clay (number 23).

The good news?

In 1988, ten Kentucky counties made the top twenty-five.

That six of the seven in–state top twenty-five poorest U.S. counties are in eastern Kentucky adds to the dubious distinction. Despite the obvious progress made in the mountains over recent decades, the time–worn negative stereotypes won't ever go away until the talking stops and the working starts.

Elliott County, for one, *is* working, involving local residents in plans for a new major tourism–based development that hinges on state and federal funding and highway improvement, a project that is finally getting lukewarm support and attention from Frankfort.

And, to be honest, census statistics are a little misleading. They can't factor in the variations in the cost of living, for one thing: A resourceful rural eastern Kentucky family with a garden, woodpile, and a healthy dose of self-sufficiency can stretch a dollar a lot further than can an urban family in a housing project.

That difference makes sheer survival a little more likely, but it doesn't change the reality that pockets of eastern Kentucky are still landlocked by bad roads, sometimes hindered by local leadership, and virtually ignored by agencies such as the Appalachian Regional Commission and Kentucky's economic development offices.

Ron Eller suggests a focus on "distressed communities" within the high-ranking counties, the pockets where as much as 60 percent of the population lives below the national poverty level, and I wish somebody would listen to him.

Study after study confirms the grim reality. Agency after agency offers lip service then plows its funding into the areas with the most political clout.

We need a governor committed to doing something about those seven counties. We need another Bert Combs. Another Carl Perkins in Washington.

Another Harry Caudill to flog the politicians and corporate moguls.

Nobody can deny the progress that has been made in the mountains over the past forty years—the highways and hospitals, factories and shopping centers, water lines and sewer systems.

Forty years ago the shotgun approach worked. Aim aid at any place east of Winchester and watch the results.

Now, obviously, it's time to focus on the "distressed communities."

One simple goal? To remove those seven Kentucky counties from the U.S. top twenty-five listings.

To address the imbalance between Woodford County's $24,493 per capita income and McCreary County's $7,663.

What's missing in many eastern Kentucky counties is the mass of middle-income families common to the flatter, more industrialized regions. As Ron Eller says, there is "significant variation" within the income levels of the poorest counties.

What that means, in simple language, is that the rich get richer and the poor get poorer.[41]

Stranger than Truth

The only thing I ever wanted to be was a writer.

A writer of fiction, of short stories and novels, the stuff of imagination and fascination.

My only formal preparation was a single creative-writing course, in 1963, at Berea College.

For the fifteen years immediately following graduation, the writing I did was totally technical, journalistic, or—increasingly—in the essay form.

But for some reason, in late 1979, I realized that if I was to ever write fiction I'd better get started.

There were a few minor handicaps.

I couldn't type, didn't own a typewriter.

I was pushing forty and had never submitted a short story to a magazine.

I did not have the almost prerequisite degree from Iowa, Hollins, or one of the other handful of "writing" schools, the almost mandatory academic credentials for New York literary recognition.

I had no money, no way to pay the bills while I took time for creative writing, no earthly concept of just what I was getting myself into.

I did it anyhow.

Resigned from my job, sort of survived by working as a consultant and copywriter, borrowed a typewriter, and pecked out craft/travel features for such publications as *Michigan Living, Chevron USA, Ohio Motorist, Grit,* and *The Crafts Report.*

And I wrote fiction for the first time since college.

"The Breeding," a coarse and brutal short story, appeared under the byline "Jack Parker" when it ran in *Cavalier* magazine in July 1981.

At the very last minute, I used the pseudonym for fiction in a magazine known mostly for its pornographic photo spreads. And I almost refused to cash the two-hundred-dollar check, thinking I might keep it as a souvenir.

Almost.

I settled for a framed photocopy and used the money to pay overdue bills.

Cavalier wanted more fiction, but made it clear that complex characters and plots were unwanted. Give us two explicit sex scenes per story, the editor told me, and keep it simple, stupid.

Don't interfere with the photo spreads.

I started over, under my own name. Quit trying to be Harold Robbins. Reread everything "Appalachian" I could get my hands on.

Wrote. And wrote, and wrote.

I discovered quickly that contemporary publishers had no interest whatsoever in the fiction I wrote, the characters and backdrops I used, the skimpy-but-blunt writing style that avoids ever going inside a character's head to explain why he or she does something.

The authors who've certainly influenced my work are a diverse lot: Hemingway, from the time I can remember reading, for his lean and taut style; nearby and much-loved Jesse Stuart, to whom I'm most often compared; mystery writer John D. MacDonald; historian Bruce Catton; Mickey Spillane and Zane Gray; and, always, O. Henry, whose short stories about rascals, shop girls, and noble derelicts I've been reading and rereading for more than forty years.

Harriette Arnow helped provide direction and inspiration; for technique, I turn to my old friends and favorites.

For stories I turned to my memories, to a tiny pocket of northeast Kentucky, to everyday life, family and friends, to the people I know, understand, and love most of all.

The stories poured out.

I built up an impressive rejection file. *Harper's* editor Lewis Lapham offered the most encouragement, but reported that the younger editors outvoted him, that they failed to see anything beyond rural humor in my work. They found nothing "meaningful."

To survive, I took a job with MATCH, Inc., opening a craft warehouse in Berea.

That summer dry weather in the Kentucky mountains forced the copperhead snakes down off the higher levels, down to the lakes, ponds, creeks, wells, and people, and the frequent near-lethal encounters triggered *Copperhead Summer*, my bawdy tale of serpent handlers, a has-been basketball star, and the complicated hero's homecoming to Cox County, Kentucky.

I learned how much work is involved in writing a book-length manuscript. How drained a writer can be when it's over. How good it feels to finish a drawn-out project.

I mailed *Copperhead Summer* to Avon Books. Unsolicited, unagented. After four or five months, I called New York and identified myself.

"Oh," exclaimed the lady who answered the phone. "You wrote *Copperhead Summer*."

I almost fainted.

"You've made it through the first three readings," she reported. "In about a week you'll get the official report."

Stunned, stumbling, I mentally made plans on how I'd spend all the money and deal with all the literary accolades headed my way.

The letter came in two weeks. In it were the words that were to become so horribly familiar. "Too regional."

But, curiously, the same letter suggested revisions to include more "folklore," more of what people expect from Appalachian fiction, more stereotype and local color. More of what I get accused of using too much.

My publishing efforts were bolstered when, in an icy grocery store parking lot, Oscar Rucker asked me if I'd write a crafts book for his Kentucke Imprints press.

I declined. But I did mention that I had on hand a series of short stories. Oscar, whose specialty is historic reprints, politely agreed to take a look.

To my shock, he called back within the week with an offer to publish *Fire on the Mountain*.

Berea College professor Bill Best added to the shock. He'd read the stories and wanted me to appear on a panel with him during the conference of the Appalachian Writers Association (AWA) in Johnson City, Tennessee.

A panel on humor in Appalachian literature.

I hedged.

Sidney Farr almost literally dragged me to the 1982 AWA conference. She scheduled me to read during a session she convened.

There I first met Sharyn McCrumb, Jim Wayne Miller, Mona K. Helper, Jack Higgs, and many of the others who were to provide so much support through such troubled times.

For the coming months were the bottom of the barrel for me. In October 1982, a grand jury indictment accused me of forgery, a leftover accusation from my years as director of the Kentucky Guild of Artists and Craftsmen. The funding for my job with MATCH ended. Publication of *Fire on the Mountain* was delayed. I was accused, blackballed, broke, and given a firsthand inside look at Kentucky's county jails when I could not keep up with child-support payments.

On a forgettable February Saturday, home alone in a cold, gray drizzle, the postman added to my gloom by delivering three new rejections.

I tossed the three manuscripts into the open fireplace.

Liked the flaming result.

Went for more fuel.

A bottle of bourbon and the burning of at least a thousand typed pages occupied the entire Saturday afternoon. I finally went for the typewriter, to add plastic and metal to the inferno and forever remove the temptation to write, but was too plastered by then to unplug and move the black portable.

I passed out on the hearth, luckily didn't burn down our house or anybody else's.

The next months are a painful blur.

But in November 1983, *Fire on the Mountain* was finally published. Two thousand copies, 133 pages, a thin paperback with the scowling author pictured on the back cover.

If ever any human being ever needed a ray of light and hope, I needed *Fire on the Mountain.*

The slim little book probably saved my life.

I shared a Kentucky Book Fair booth with best-selling fiction author Stephen Birmingham. Reviews were positive. A job offer came from Morehead State University's Appalachian Development Center. In the Spring, Peggy Gabriel used "The Liberation of Elsie Watts," from the new book, as part of an Appalachian literature feature in *The Mountain Spirit,* the magazine of the Christian Appalachian Project. Over four hundred book orders poured in. Jack Hicks wrote a feature for the *Kentucky Post.* "The Liberation of Elsie Watts" won first place in the Catholic Press Association's national fiction competition, and the same story was chosen for Rudy Thomas's teaching anthology *The Uneven Ground.*

Working in Morehead, living away from home during the week, barely surviving from one paycheck to the next was a surprisingly productive time. I took graduate courses, taught a creative-writing class for high school students, helped revive the Appalachian Writers Association, staged a conference—which was Harriette Arnow's final appearance as a speaker—on campus, and won awards for the short story "Big Game" and the poem "Come Home."

I wrote "Hellcat" for *Appalachian Heritage,* "A Matter of Vision" for *The Mountain Spirit,* and twenty more short stories that were to become, in 1986, the Kentucke Imprints book *Mountain Passage & Other Stories.*

But I'd already moved back to Berea full time when, in late 1985, my novel *Copperhead Summer* was published by Kentucke Imprints. I learned, in the process, what Ernest Hemingway meant when he said what was left out was as important as what was used; I cut seventy-five pages from the typeset galleys, an expensive and much-needed improvement to my first novel. Then, in 1988, a third short story collection, *All Night Dog,* was led off by three stories originally published in *The Mountain,* a short-lived Galax, Virginia, attempt at a general-interest Appalachian magazine.

I collected my free-verse poetry into *Bitter Creek Breakdown,* and the chapbook has sold over a thousand copies.

My workload and other projects—hosting Berea conferences of the Appalachian Studies Association and the Appalachian Writers Association, finally completing *The Handcraft Revival in Southern Appalachia, 1930–1990,* which was published by the University of Tennessee Press, helping rebuild the Berea College Student Crafts Program—have shoved fiction to a back burner during recent years, and a lack of interest from national publishers has perhaps dulled the competitive edge.

What I consider my best work of fiction—the novel *Gum-*

bottom—is on the waiting list for a rewrite after marketing staff overruled the editors at Ballantine Books and vetoed the recommended publication.

"Too regional," said the people who sell the books, and who the hell is Garry Barker? Ditto for a proposed short story collection at the same publishing house, despite strong support from the managing editor.

The familiar old fear of a native voice, unshaped by professional tutoring, still interferes with publication.

So my writing efforts have turned to other directions. But, even after *The Handcraft Revival in Southern Appalachia,* controversy snips at credibility; many critics continue to have difficulty dealing with an outspoken, unscholarly way of working, with an unschooled, mountain-reared, noncredentialed practitioner who wrote an unconventional history.

I get reviewed more often than does the book.

A pair of as yet unpublished mysteries are the net fiction output of the past two years. And, to the surprise of many, including me, I have not written a decent short story in three years.

There have been a few recent bright spots: a private school in Louisville uses *Mountain Passage* as a text; a western Kentucky high school uses *Copperhead Summer.* My favorite short story, "Hellcat," was chosen for *Groundwater,* a new Kentucky fiction anthology, and "Kaiser" will be part of the new two-volume Higgs-Manning-Miller anthology, *Appalachia Inside Out* (University of Tennessee Press, 1995).

My fiction is still raw, bawdy, fast-paced, and as regional as ever, still as unacceptable and unworthy as it has always been in academic circles.

I simply do not, can not, write subtle, witty, literary fiction with lots of allusions to the classics.

My fiction, I'm afraid, is more like me.

Unpolished, rowdy, sentimental, a little out of control, the product of a half century of life on the edge, halfway between mountain tradition and modern middle-class values.

So be it.

I write what I know, feel, remember, and see.

I am what I am.

Part 2

Working

I Still Love to Mow

We cropped a farm at Bluebank, grew five acres of burley tobacco on the halves, and did it all with horses. Three teams—big-footed draft horses with fat backs and sweaty harnesses—pulled the plows and wagons and disk harrow. I turned new ground with a three-horse hitch, worked off their winter fat, then rode the water tank of the tobacco setter and raced down the rows on a foot-guided sulky cultivator.

At daylight I harnessed the teams, stood on a wooden box to reach across the powerful shoulders and flanks, crawled under their bellies to fasten the snaps and buckles, and loved the huge, gentle animals who served so faithfully.

Summers, between work on the tobacco, we mowed. A pair of well-greased John Deere mowers, rattling pitman rods and chattering cutting bars, weeds and briars and fescue falling in orderly precision, two hundred acres to mow at seven acres a day.

My team was a pair of matched grays, Kate and Beck, sensitive souls who set their own pace, nipped my shoulders when I turned my back, rolled and played like clumsy oversized puppies at the end of the day. We spent six or seven summers together, marking off a land and circling until all the weeds were gone.

I still love to mow. You can see where you've been.[1]

Working

My first real job, in 1961, was with the Flemingsburg Lumber Company.

I had good reason to ask there first for employment: my father already worked there as a carpenter, and my first girlfriend was the owner's daughter.

My hiring was an early lesson in differing expectations.

I wanted work in construction, in the manly building of barns, laying of cement blocks, the building of new houses from footers to finish cabinetry. I was willing to dry-stack the heavy oak timbers, dig deep ditches, unload the 120-pound bags of cement, drive a dump truck, cut glass, thread plumbing pipe.

I saw myself as a rugged seventeen-year-old ready laborer, lean and mean, all set to work, spit, sweat, swear, and share in the low-paid masculine satisfaction of doing work with visible results.

My new boss saw me a little differently.

He saw the high school honors graduate, the student-body president and prom king, the college-bound young leader, the potential white-collar administrator who'd earned the break he was ready to give to me.

He needed, he said, an office worker. A sales clerk, an inventory manager, a person to help with the administrative side of the complex construction business.

Right then what I needed, beyond any doubt, was a job.

So I took it. At seventy-five cents an hour.

Forced myself to greet customers and offer cheery assistance. Learned how to write up sales tickets and use the cash register; learned how to prepare the orders for the hardware vendors who came by weekly.

In less than a week I had totally cleaned and reorganized the warehouse, glass room, nail and bolt areas, paint displays, and everything else inside the building.

What I could not learn, could not deal with, was the open scorn from the other lumberyard workers, their perception that I was the owner's pet, a coddled youngster unwilling and unable to pull my own weight.

I asked for a change, dumbly threatened to quit if I didn't get to do some real work, gratefully compromised on a split week: three days in the office, three days in the yard or on work crews.

By summer's end I *was* the lean and brown construction worker I'd envisioned, and I'd done all the things I thought the real men did. I earned my respect at the everyday cost of calluses, aching muscles, blisters, total exhaustion, miles of sewer trenches, and endless truckloads of lumber, Sheetrock, cement, and iron pipe.

I'd also gained a creeping new appreciation for the air-conditioned office and retail-sales area, for the physically easier life of a white-collar employee.

I went strutting off to college in September, only to discover that not one of my new skills was of any earthly use to me at Berea. Nor were all my enlarged muscles, except when it was time to lug 16mm army surplus movie projectors up and down stairs.

On my Berea College placement tests I'd scored high on what they then called "mechanical ability" and had been offered a job in the school's Audio Visual Service via a registered letter in midsummer. I carried the letter to a neighbor, a Berea graduate, and asked for advice.

"On your application, what kind of work did you tell them you'd done before?" he asked.

I'd told the truth. Farm labor.

"Do you want to milk cows in college?" he asked.

I took the AVS job.

A week after I hit campus, though, I knew I'd made a serious mistake.

Cows I could have handled.

Now, not only was I expected to work twelve hours a week operating and maintaining machines I'd never known existed, to show classroom films for exacting, intimidating professors, and memorize a Standard Operations Procedures manual at least an inch thick, but also I was working for a *woman.*

A woman who didn't wear aprons, didn't make biscuits, didn't change diapers, didn't iron my clothes or cut me any slack.

Louise Gibson was—at first—an ogre, a demanding perfectionist, the master of expecting too much and getting what she expected.

From a handpicked crew of student workers who were paid wages of fifteen to thirty-four cents per hour.

Students who came from tiny mountain communities and who came in astounding varieties of weird, eccentric, and wonderful.

After I survived the initial shock, and after she made a few adaptations to my strange and stubborn ways, I worked for Louise for three school years and part of a fourth and bought into her concept that we were the elite corps on campus.

Back home for the summer after my freshman year, I was sent to dig up a drain line from the basement of newly built house to the city main fifty yards away. It took two days, two of us with picks and shovels in the mud and sweltering heat.

The lady of the house vented her anger at the clogged drain on Frank and me, treated us like two subhuman, feelingless, uncivilized morons, watched us closely to make sure, I guess, that we didn't steal or damage any of her mud or let our pungent aroma drift too near her elegant new home.

The second day I wore a tattered Berea College sweatshirt. At mid-morning, I realized the woman was near the trench, peering down at me.

"Where," she asked tightly, "did you get that shirt?"

The implication seemed to be that I'd surely stolen it.

I bit my lip and said, ever so politely, "I got the shirt where I go to college, Ma'am."

She squinted. "*You* go to Berea?"

I wiped some of the mud off my forehead and nodded. "I'll be a sophomore in September."

Suddenly I became a human, to her. She brought fresh lemonade. Wanted to know all about my classes, my work, the crafts, the Boone Tavern Hotel.

Instead of an animal down in a muddy ditch, I was now a

somebody. But I brought Frank up too, bulging muscles, scars, mud, and sweat, for a glass of her icy lemonade. Enjoyed her discomfort at his menacing presence.

Hated her, just then, for the judgments she was making about the two of us, the condescending value she suddenly placed on my noble effort to lift myself up from my defective surroundings.

But I played the game. Bashful, humble, hardworking Berea College student.

It was—and still is to some degree—a game most Berea students played effortlessly.

In a way we really *were* an elite, special group, handpicked from a flood of low-income, high-ability applicants. I, for one, made good use of the public's perception of us: it was always good for a quick ride when I went hitchhiking, plus sometimes meals and spending money. It all depended on how guilty the driver felt about being so well off when we weren't.

This day, though, I extracted only her tolerance of Frank's presence. Got him his share of lemonade, plus grudging permission to sit as long as I sat. After four summers on construction crews and four years of movie projectors, my work/learning program ended.

My very best recommendation, when it came time to go job hunting after college, came from Berea College AVS supervisor Louise Gibson. So did the best advice. "After you graduate," she said, "you want a career, not a job."

I took her advice to heart, declined offers of careers in selling insurance and federal civil service and was seriously considering going back home to the construction business when things took an unexpected turn.

I became a so-called "arts administrator" mostly by accident, by taking a first job out of college that grew quickly into more than was ever intended or expected.

In 1965, Southern Highland Handicraft Guild director Bob Gray needed an assistant, what he called a "leg man," and I needed a job.

But, strangely enough, I now needed—at twenty-one, in debt, ignorant, and unsettled—a job that actually *meant* something. After four years of half-hearted study, a lifetime of doing without, and a cavalier attitude toward the do-gooders of the world, something changed.

Maybe the stirrings that were to emerge years later in written form had begun; I suddenly took my half-jesting pledge to never live north of the Ohio River to heart, I was finally (I thought) free to be my own person, and for some reason the thought of a conventional job and life simply scared the hell out of me.

So I moved to Asheville, North Carolina, into the world where I've worked for all these years, into a subculture that both affirmed and denied the basic worth of the Appalachian heritage.

An organization, a force, a regional movement that valued mountain crafts, it was the first substantial group I'd ever come across that valued *anything* Appalachian.

And, to be honest, I'd never particularly valued the crafts.

I grew up sleeping under a quilting frame suspended from the bedroom ceiling, sitting in handmade chairs, wearing handmade clothes. My grandfathers were cobblers, blacksmiths, gunsmiths, and woodworkers by necessity, and my father worked as a carpenter.

But, like almost everybody else I knew, I would have preferred to have the store-bought stuff.

The guild, though, used crafts to generate income for mountain craftspeople. This was not, I was to soon learn, a brand-new concept; Berea College had used crafts as an economic factor since 1893, and the guild's work dated back to 1928. I'd managed to spend four years in Berea without ever really noticing the craftwork being done there, but I really had gone off to school with the idea of getting *away* from working with my hands.

But I had not been hired to weave or make pots. I was the staff writer (of press releases, newsletters, and brochure copy), and I was Bob Gray's extended administrative arm. Quickly I was immersed in craft fairs, retail selling, public speaking, printing and photography, educational workshops, and travel promotion; by default, I became the guild's auto and building-maintenance person, purchasing agent, carpenter, delivery person, janitor, and in-house muscle for the never-ending lifting, loading, and packing that is such a part of the craft world at any level.

All of that was okay by me. I knew *how* to lift, hammer, drive, and paint, and sometimes a familiar physical task was a welcome relief from all the learning.

For Bob Gray was a teacher and an intense, no-nonsense organizer and administrator who emphasized preparation, hard work, and creative solutions. His dry sense of humor, stubborn combativeness, and uncanny ability to cut through the smoke screens to get to the heart of an issue set him apart from anyone I've ever worked with, before or since. He surely gambled on me and risked his success by assuming that the best way for me to learn was by doing. He'd give me overall direction, pick up the pieces and patch the wounds when I made mistakes, and he only got angry if I made the same error twice.

Bob found ways to supplement my laughable salary and to see that I participated in workshops, regional and national meetings, planning sessions, budgeting, and whatever else was part of the guild's work. My ideas were encouraged and frequently implemented; I was made part of overall management in a way few new college graduates are ever lucky enough to experience.

Bob Gray never rested, never stopped working, and for over five years I was one of his projects. He smoothed many of my rough edges, brought my temper under control (by calmly pointing out that losing control usually means losing the battle), carefully saved his criticisms and reprimands for when we were alone, accepted but never approved of my motorcycle riding, poker playing, golf, and guns.

We were an unlikely combination, the brash but hesitant young Kentuckian and the calm, controlled Floridian, but it worked. We *could* disagree, especially on matters "Appalachian," where his was a clinical, dispassionate appraisal and mine was an emotional, inside-out personal struggle. Bob loathed the massive waste of the antipoverty movement and firmly believed that anyone who wanted to improve themselves could do so through simple self-discipline and hard work.

I wanted to believe that but really couldn't.

Bob Gray was a conservative Republican; I was a liberal Democrat.

What prevented outright clashes was Bob's profound respect for the Appalachian culture, admittedly for the more quaint aspects, but there was also a total compassion for the low-income craftspeople struggling to survive.

Bob also understood the quick, close friendships I found with the native craftspeople, those whose backgrounds I shared, those of us who communicate instantly without words.

But, even in 1965, those native craftspeople were a distinct minority.

The guild's mixed message dates back to its very beginnings. One strong voice says "preserve the native traditions, create income for needy people, promote appreciation for local skills passed down through the generations."

The other voice, stronger and more educated, says "change, improve, upgrade, learn better design and more sophisticated methods, move beyond your roots, and become part of the modern craft world."

Long before David Whisnant challenged a hundred years of Appalachian cultural missionary work in his book *All That Is Native and Fine,* I was getting a mixed message from inside that very movement. Honor tradition, support production, and build business, said one side of the guild; be artists, rise above the conventional, cast aside old restrictions, said the other.

Strangely enough, at that time, in that place, it worked. Because of the people involved—Clem Douglas, O. J. Mattil, Marian Heard, Lucy Morgan, and the many other longtime leaders—who were always giving and never taking, always concerned that they not be condescending to native artisans, the contradictory directions didn't often cause open conflict.

Not everyone, including me, saw the "missionary" intervention as all good. And Henry D. Shapiro wrote, in 1976, about what he termed "Appalachian otherness": a geographic and ethnic separation characterized by the "folk" who lived here during the early 1900s.

"If folk culture was the creation of the folk," wrote Shapiro, "then all mountain people must be song-singers and tale-tellers, shingle-makers and weavers, dyers and basket-makers, in potential if not in practice."[2]

So, according to Shapiro, the early outsiders—missionaries and educators—proceeded to attempt to force us to become ourselves, as they perceived us, to evolve backwards into the quaint "folk" the world wanted to believe still existed in Appalachian America. They wanted us to again be, I assume, what they thought we were back before we embraced our evil ways, before we picked up on the dastardly fiddle and banjo, the mail-order catalog, the jenny barn and the Colt revolver.

Those who are of the mountains still exhibit the "otherness" Henry Shapiro wrote about, and back then we were quick to latch onto the crafts as a means of earning a living. We've kept the myth alive, too, turned it into practical reality, used it to build a multi-million-dollar crafts marketplace.

The years I lived and worked in Asheville I was generally known as "the Kentuckian," so strong is my attachment to home, so it didn't really surprise anyone when I came back, to run Berea College's retail shops, in 1970. I was surprised that I simply could not fit into Berea's administrative system—the ponderous, committee-based, turf-protecting style so common to institutions—and I quickly left the stifling security of the campus for the haphazard, harder, but infinitely more exciting job as director of the Kentucky Guild of Artists and Craftsmen.

The college's miffed personnel director wrote in my file that I was "totally unsuited to the corporate structure." I thanked him for the compliment and went to work.

The younger, smaller, less-established Kentucky Guild, by virtue of having less to lose, was more willing to try new directions and take chances, which we did with major success and failure for the next ten years. I was swept—willingly at first—into a different world of politics, openings and receptions, fund-raising and education.

To better play the role of arts administrator I let my hair grow long, adopted wire-rimmed glasses, leather jackets, and boots as my working uniform, and lived up to the expectation that a Kentucky crafts promoter, operating more often on promise than substance, should be slightly outrageous, outspoken, colorful, and eccentric.

Much of the time I had no earthly idea just what the "art" we were promoting really meant; the paintings, sculpture, and unpleasant abstract craft forms that require a lengthy written explanation and justification seemed to me to be lacking in something very basic. But I went along with it all. As in the old fable about the emperor's new clothes, people tend to believe what they're told, and sometimes even those who do the telling and create the artificial reality start believing. So I made sure we put on a good show and maintained the outward image of creative excitement.

Under the surface there was hard work, organization, total dedication, creative insecurity, and a stubborn determination to turn concepts into reality.

Our Berea craft fairs were, throughout most of a decade, *the* craft events to thousands of visitors and customers. The planned festive atmosphere of art, crafts, food, dancers, music, crowds, and free-spirited fun was fueled by the era of flower children, disenchanted yuppies, free-flowing state and federal funding, and a contagious outdoor celebration of art, nature, and human spirit.

I loved it. I worked around the clock and around the calendar to keep it all happening, and was unexpectedly rewarded with a national prominence in the flourishing craft world. I was asked to judge shows, serve as a consultant, write for craft magazines, speak, travel, and assume a leadership role in the craft profession.

It was, I thought, just what I'd always wanted.

But the glamour was shallow, the internal struggles too personal and bitter.

My bias toward serving the traditional Kentucky craftspeople and the growing number of professionals—whose livelihood depended upon sales—was in perpetual conflict with those more educated and vocal guild members whose loftier organizational goal was "art." Education, as I saw the guild's role, was more a matter of skill and business training than of the nebulous, expensive art education already being offered by the colleges and universities.

I fought off moves to ban the production centers, which primarily served low-income eastern Kentuckians (and whose sales financed the more elegant exhibits and workshops) from the guild.

I grew more and more weary of fighting the same old battles over and over, of always having to compromise my basic feelings, of being damned if I did and damned if I didn't

A much-pruned section (salvaged from the original full chapter titled "Damned if you do") from *The Handcraft Revival in*

Southern Appalachia, 1930–1990, deals with the arts administrator's nearly impossible role, with the mixed expectations a guild director must fulfill:

> No guild director ever has an easy life, and today's high-volume sales make solid management even more crucial. The ideal craft guild administrator would have the hide of an alligator, the wisdom of Moses, the business acumen and luck of Lee Iacocca, Lyndon Johnson's political skills, the arrogant generalship of a Douglas MacArthur, the steely nerves of a riverboat gambler, a private fortune, and the soul of a free-spirited artist. . . .
>
> It is the nature of an arts membership organization to periodically dissolve into backstabbing, bickering and wailing, and vicious infighting. One constant, the one predictable factor, is that paid staff will be blamed for any shortcomings of elected leadership.
>
> In most organizations, the paid executive has both too much and too little power. The "too much" covers day-to-day operations, usually with little or no guidance from the elected directors. Far too often, the executive makes decisions on directions, goals, and image which should be made by a larger group from the membership. The other side of this coin is the elected officer who wants total daily involvement, who would like to direct every small detail without assuming any overall responsibility.
>
> An executive's "too little" authority comes when every decision is subject to reversal, when continued employment is subject more to popularity than to competence. Elected officers frequently resent the high visibility of the paid administrator, and the tenuous relationship can become very strained. I do not see significant changes taking place within the craft organizations regarding staff-board relationships. The administrator's position is still precarious, political, and torn between two elements. The very same job which requires flair, imagination, and the gambler's instinct also needs conservative, stolid management. It's hard to go in both directions at the same time, hard to both lead

> and follow. There are few familiar faces left from my years in guild administration. Most of us have moved on to more stable and less painful positions; new faces are fighting the same old battles.
>
> The situation isn't likely to change in Appalachia. We are in one sense more production oriented, more traditional in product, more geared toward the craft "center," but the individual craftspeople continue to develop in both directions, toward art and toward business, with enough success both ways to keep everyone busy. Private enterprise has grown into a large part of the marketing role once filled by the guilds, and the reality that guild membership is no longer crucial to financial survival has lessened the tensions to some degree.[3]

I was, I began to realize early in 1979, very out of place in the world of artists and art educators. I was hungry for something more real, less artificial, a world more of people than of pretense and puffery.

So I quit in 1980. With no real plans, no money, no idea of how I'd survive, but with a naive belief that I would write, somehow return to my roots, simply shift gears, and begin a new career.

Wrong.

An almost forty-year-old, eccentric, big-mouthed former arts administrator is not exactly a marketable commodity in the real world. And my writing was usually too regional, too controversial, too far out of the mainstream to generate any significant income.

Without my former job title, the lucrative consultant contracts were no longer available.

My belief that I'd just work at a nonmanagement level, use my back instead of my brains, then write at night went quickly out the window when every prospective employer told me I was overeducated, overqualified, and—maybe the biggest shock—too old.

The real world, I soon found out, does not value prior success in the art and craft arena.

They're probably correct; anyone unconventional enough to succeed in art administration probably *is* unsuited to the corporate structure.

I took a series of jobs, including one as a manager of the Appalachian Book and Record Shop, a Council of the Southern Mountains project in chronic disarray.

It was a lost cause. There was no money to pay publishers, no credit, no way to fill the many orders on hand, no escape from the bitter struggles within the council that were the cause of the problems.

It *was* an opportunity to read and reread the literature of the region and to meet many of the contemporary authors of Appalachia. It was also the beginning of a collaborative effort with a passionate, young artist, Mitchell Tolle, the writing of the first short "sketches" about life in rural eastern Kentucky that were to become, twelve years later, part of the text for *Mitchell Tolle: American Artist.*

An initial grant from Berea College's Appalachian Center helped me get started on my Appalachian craft history.

I declined the offer to stay on at the bookstore after six months; I had no desire to oversee the final collapse.

My first book was published in 1983. *Fire on the Mountain* solidly delivered a heritage, a viewpoint, a confirmation of my Appalachian roots. Many readers who'd known me only as the multifaceted arts administrator were puzzled to discover my true background. Some readers who gave me so much credit for having a "good ear" for dialect and for having researched well didn't know I wrote totally from personal experience and instinct.

The new book, the many brochures and catalogs, and the rapidly growing Berea Craft Festival nudged open new employment doors; in early 1984 I was hired as communications coordinator for Morehead State University's Appalachian Development Center.

The first day, I declined the offer to coordinate the craft market that was part of the annual Appalachian Celebration. I was, I explained, out of the craft world, forever, except for the Berea show.

That was not to be.

Despite my new success in writing, I could not completely leave the world of crafts. Too many old friends called, too many struggling producers needed help, too many newspapers called for background information and valid statistics.

And there was that nagging unfinished project, my Appalachian craft history.

Morehead State University was then in the midst of its musical chairs succession of presidents, a chaotic time for campus personnel and politics, and there came a proposal to relocate me from the Appalachian Development Center to the university's information office. I didn't want to go.

And, for over a year, I had been quietly recruited by Berea College to work in their student crafts department, to be part of major restructuring about to begin.

I finally accepted, knowing there'd be some leftover flak.

Word of my hiring did trigger some Berea resistance, some old rumors and accusations, some open attempts to block my employment, and surely some trepidation from those who'd once worked so hard to see that I was destroyed.

There was also, thankfully, much relief and a warm welcome from those who wanted me back.

Essentially, I came to work for Berea College under probation, complete with not-so-subtle warnings to tone down my working style, to control my opinionated assessments, to adjust and adapt to the workings of an institution that has to carefully guard its public image.

I stepped on the president's toes during our initial meeting. He directed me to emphasize all that was "Appalachian" in the product line, and I allowed as how that'd be real easy since there were no true Appalachian crafts being made at the college.

My point was, simply, that Berea College effectively preserves a tradition, not a product. We do not quilt, make cornshuck dolls, weave willow baskets, or whittle out figurines; we *do* emphasize quality and the intrinsic values of hand skills, natural materials, and the satisfaction of a job well done.

The response to my Berea College presence from the two craft guilds that have been such a large part of my life was an amusing contrast: in Asheville, the Southern Highland Handicraft Guild welcomed me with open arms; in Berea, the Kentucky Guild apprehensively waited for the trouble to start.

They're still waiting. And maybe still wondering why I dissolved my association with the Berea Craft Festival.

The college staff, once the shock of seeing me there wore off, accepted and appreciated the hard work, emphasis on quality, and willingness to accept responsibility and implement change that I helped bring to the Student Crafts Program.

For the first time in my career, I could function as a business manager instead of having every decision subject to a mass vote. Part of my split personality is a love for marketing, for efficiency and accomplishment, and for what some regard as hard-nosed administration. The apparent conflict, between creativity and organization, works well; much of my work in printing, copy writing, ad design, and product development draws on creative surges, but we also have a business to run, and I enjoy the computers, projections, and the challenge of helping make a handcraft business largely staffed by students actually function.

For me, Berea also offers rewards outside the daily work world. I am free to write, to be involved in many things "Appalachian" other than crafts, to teach sometimes, to share in the overall process of education and regional service.

My faded jeans, editorial writing, humor, and bias toward what I consider real Appalachian people and values can still cause friction on campus. My finally completed Appalachian craft history did revive some old unpleasantness; the writing of that study was, for me, excellent mental therapy, the spelling out of old frustrations and hurts, and anyone who thinks the published version is too personal should have seen the early drafts.

My inside-out view of Appalachia, my insistence that real people are more important than published studies, can still rattle the cages.

I've had to learn new methods, new craft markets, and new directions, from direct mail to international sales, from subcontracting to the impersonal world of trade shows. I serve on faculty committees and councils, statewide and regional boards, and advisory panels. In 1994, after serving as interim director for the third time, I was made director of the Student Crafts Program.

A term on the Board of Trustees of the Southern Highland Handicraft Guild let me see the other side of crafts administration: the tightrope act of overseeing a director and staff, the pressures and politics of maintaining one of this nation's oldest and largest craft programs.

In 1992 the guild surprised me with a Life Membership, that

organization's major recognition of a member's contributions, the honor I cherish above any other.

I continue to write, speak, argue, entertain, travel, learn, and work.

My two worlds—crafts and writing—coexist with minimum friction, sometimes even overlap, and after so many years I still love the working craftspeople and the things they make, the traditions and the new directions.

I still am surprised to find I'm often considered a crafts "expert," but I suspect that has more to do with years than actual knowledge.

It *has* been a long time since 1965, since my first awkward steps into the Appalachian craft world, and on some days the pain and frustration outweigh the wonders. But, still, sometimes there's an almost magical, childlike delight with the world and all it has to offer, and a richer understanding of what North Carolina handweaver Granny Jude meant almost a hundred years ago when she exclaimed, "Shucks, ain't it grand, the things they is to do and find out about."[4]

Yes, indeed, Granny. I know exactly what you mean.

Writing about the Crafts

Over the past thirty years I have, obviously, written often about the mountain crafts world, from a column on administration for *The Crafts Report* to exhibition reviews for the old *Craft Horizons*, plus a series of "think" pieces for regional journals.

Much of that writing was pulled together in *The Handcraft Revival in Southern Appalachia, 1930–1990.*

But the writing, speaking, and thinking never stops.

In 1989 I was asked to come to New York and speak to the Saudi-U.S. Cultural Heritage Conference to explain to a hall filled with folklorists, economic developers, Saudi princes, and Ph.D. specialists just how such a poor and isolated mountain region had essentially created a marketplace that had in turn helped preserve a traditional culture.

For the New York University presentation, I wrote "Appalachian Crafts: What Role Has the Marketplace Played in Preserving the Culture?"

In America's southern Appalachian Mountains, physical isolation preserved the native craft culture for more than 150 years. When change did come—roadways, manufacturing, mail order—and began to eliminate the need for the hand skills involved in quilting, basketry, woodworking, and pottery, a missionary effort directly tied to the marketplace took over and preserved a vanishing culture.

Berea College in Kentucky began its unique crafts-for-education barter system in 1893. Handwoven coverlets from Appalachia were sold to the college's New England supporters and soon the demand was so large that full-time marketing specialist was employed. In 1896, Berea staged its first Homespun Fair, an event that drew weavers, chair makers, and basket makers from the surrounding mountains to the campus for a full day of swapping and selling.

At the same time, in the mountains near Asheville, North Carolina, Presbyterian missionary worker Frances Goodrich also worked to revive the handcrafts, primarily handweaving. Goodrich opened a shop, Allanstand, to sell the work. Today Allanstand is part of the Southern Highland Folk Art Center on the Blue Ridge Parkway near Asheville. In 1989, sales of handcrafts in that shop alone exceeded one million dollars.

In tiny Gatlinburg, Tennessee, soon to become a booming resort when the Great Smoky Mountains National Park was created, the Pi Beta Phi sorority incorporated crafts training and marketing into its educational programs. The John C. Campbell Folk School in Brasstown, North Carolina, started selling the work of its local woodcarvers in 1921. For the first twenty-five years of this century, Appalachian settlement schools, colleges, individuals, and church missionary efforts worked to preserve and revive a culture, and their primary preservation tool was the marketplace. In a remote region with few sources of cash income, the sale of baskets, coverlets, and carvings was a major economic factor.

In 1930, the forces working to preserve the Appalachian crafts came together to form the Southern Highland Handicraft Guild, a nine-state educational and marketing cooperative that combined the many small groups into a powerful effort for both conservation and change. There was no state or federal support for this early work; the marketplace provided the funding. That early market, much as it does today, depended heavily on the tourists visiting the mountains and on selective collectors from outside the region.

There was federal support from 1935 to 1950 through the Tennessee Valley Authority (TVA), which helped create Southern Highlanders, Inc., a marketing cooperative jointly administered with the new guild. Shops were opened in New York City and in several new TVA facilities in Tennessee, and TVA training programs helped develop the skills of local woodworkers.

While this combined force of missionary effort and growing marketplace (documented in Allen H. Eaton's *Handicrafts of the Southern Highlands*) preserved the tradition of producing regional handcrafts, both forces also brought change to the local culture.

The more-educated outsiders, argues David Whisnant in his book *All That Is Native and Fine,* imposed their own values and design concepts upon the Appalachian craft culture. Berea College's first weaving instructor, in 1911, was Swedish, and the John C. Campbell Folk School was modeled after Danish folk schools, so much of the region's handweaving quickly took on a Scandinavian accent.

This "manipulation"—the redesigning of tradition to better suit the taste of those doing the organizational work—has continued, and the native Appalachian culture was diluted even more in the fifties and sixties by the influx of schooled craftspeople drawn to the region by the ready marketplace.

The sixties War on Poverty also bravely and blindly tackled craft marketing as an economic-development tool in Appalachia. This expensive fifteen-year effort proved mostly that quality is essential to craft marketing; most craft projects funded by the Office of Economic Opportunity (OEO) were staffed by eager youngsters with limited knowledge of Appalachia, cultural preservation, crafts, or business, and much of what was presented as mountain crafts was of the scrolled-aluminum-beer-can, carved-Clorox-bottle, gaudy-crocheted-afghan variety.

There were some major exceptions—Cabin Creek Quilts in West Virginia, Iron Mountain Stoneware in Tennessee, and Grass Roots Quilters in Kentucky—but the sixties developers left mostly a heritage of too much money for consultants and too little for skill training, a sixties crudeness of design and workmanship, and the wistful memory of plentiful one-hundred-dollar-a-day contracts.

The sixties did mark a new era in craft marketing. Demand exceeded supply; "natural" and "native" were "in" words, and the customer base grew to include the many young professionals disillusioned with plastic, impersonal service, and a distant, senseless war. Sales doubled almost every year between 1965 and 1970; the hoopla that wrongly presented the region as a land populated by quaint dulcimer makers and illiterate moonshiners did draw enough serious attention to solidly establish quality handcrafts as a market commodity.

Though most of the leaders of the craft movement during this century have maintained a healthy respect for local culture and have worked diligently to preserve native skills and designs, the modern Appalachian craft market leans heavily toward a more contemporary, mainstream product line, though much of the work is derived from or influenced by mountain craft traditions. At Berea College, few of the actual crafts (except weaving) perpetuate a product tradition; what is effectively preserved at Berea is the mountain tradition of working with the hands, of using quality materials and ageless skills to create works of function and quality.

The continuing tourist demand for inexpensive souvenirs led many craftspeople to production shortcuts and emphasis on gadgets that could be quickly made and easily sold. The junk market proliferated, as evidenced today in downtown Gatlinburg, Tennessee, and Cherokee, North Carolina, and in the area's many roadside stands and truck-stop gift shops. Some of the handcraft producers simply grew into manufacturing centers, such as the Three Mountaineers wood plant in Asheville, North Carolina. Other craft production centers, such as the Stuart Nye Silver Shop in Asheville and Churchill Weavers in Berea, successfully adapted the hand process to a volume output.

To offset the mass-production influence, the new guild, Berea College, and other Appalachian institutions and individuals worked to create a controlled marketplace, one where only crafts of quality would be offered, and they largely succeeded.

The region's leaders exerted their control through rigid jurying for quality and by crating outlets that sold only the very best. The Allanstand Shop in Asheville, Arrowcraft in Gatlinburg, and the Log House Sales Room in Berea were—and still are—outstanding examples of the controlled marketplace. Though Berea College's Homespun Fair did not continue, the Southern Highland Handicraft Guild's Craftsman's Fair of the Southern Highlands started in 1948 with even more emphasis on quality and tradition and has been copied in almost every Appalachian state.

The somewhat controversial quality judgments that had to be made regarding excellence preserved and built this market into a commercial success. That success kept alive the demand for excellent traditional crafts, and that demand kept alive the craft culture that places much value on quality, workmanship, and integrity.

An unmanipulated market would have soon destroyed the traditional craft culture with increased demands for low-end, inexpensive gadgets, but the guild and other organizations were able to carve out and maintain a large enough market share to assure the continuation of the tradition.

The Appalachian experience points out dramatically that the marketplace can, with directed help, contribute significantly to the preservation of traditional culture. Native craftspeople are most likely to respond to an economic stimulus; few true folk artists, those who work for the simple joy of creation, exist. Even those selected few become much more prolific when ready markets are provided, and they are much more likely to train others to meet market needs and thus assure that the necessary skills are handed down to another generation.

The North Carolina Cherokee Indians are a good example. Until strong markets were built, much of the traditional basketry, carving, and pottery work was no longer being done. During the sixties, older members of the tribe eventually did the teaching. Qualla Arts and Crafts Mutual built the sales volume for quality work, and today double-weave river cane baskets are again part of the Cherokee culture.

Craft cooperatives are still common to the Appalachian region. Craftspeople pool their efforts to create a larger market impact; the craftwork is done in the homes and brought to a central collection point for distribution.

Today the southern Appalachian market for quality crafts is probably $60 million a year. The Southern Highland Handicraft Guild's annual sales are in excess of $3 million; the Berea College volume is $1.5 million. Though a substantial portion of that volume is the sale of nontraditional crafts, a significant percentage is the work of native artisans, sales that continue to preserve the culture. In 1989, a Kentucky school, Morehead State University, had to hire a full-time marketing specialist to coordinate the growing sales of area folk art to galleries across the nation.

The marketplace is an obvious force that can effectively either preserve or homogenize a local culture. When tied to educational efforts (for both craftspeople and customers) the marketplace can be a positive influence.[5]

Romancing the Crafts

In 1992, for the Appalachian Studies Conference in Asheville, North Carolina, with the theme of "Diversity in Appalachia: Images and Realities," and with David Whisnant as keynote speaker, I wrote "The Mountain Crafts: Romancing the Marketplace."[6]

Almost exactly one hundred years ago, mountain "missionaries" were discovering the Appalachian treasure trove of crafts, that highly visible and marketable aspect of the culture that held appeal for the "outsiders" whose influence and money were needed to make things happen.

Berea College president William G. Frost was making preparations for his horseback ride through eastern Kentucky, West Virginia, east Tennessee, and western North Carolina, a summer-long journey that would result in the formation of Berea's "Fireside Industries" crafts production and marketing program. In Madison County, North Carolina, Frances Louisa Goodrich was beginning the work that would create the living legend of Allanstand Cottage Industries.

The two unconnected efforts would later come together, join with forces from Penland, Brasstown, Gatlinburg, and the other more remote mountain pockets where settlement schools were preserving an almost artificial culture, and the lasting result was to be a regional phenomenon of craft training and marketing, promotion and publicity, and plenty of what David Whisnant would later term "cultural intervention."

This conditioned, much-manipulated image of the quaint, crafts-making mountaineer has, for a century, been the cornerstone of a highly profitable Appalachian crafts marketing effort that continues today but now sells mostly the work of college-trained designer-craftspeople.

Allen Eaton concluded his famed 1937 study *Handicrafts of the Southern Highlands* with these words: "To bring these people our civilization and yet save their culture is the task in which we should all have some part. There is but one approach to this task: that is the ethical approach which seeks, before imposing its own ideals on any person or group, to draw from them the best they have to give."[7]

To draw from them their best, a jaundiced 1990s observer might conclude, then use that "best" as a marketing tool for products and a culture that bear but faint resemblance to the crafts and lifestyle of a century ago.

Perhaps the best example of the successful crafts marketing myth is the crooked-seamed brown Double Bowknot coverlet now owned by the Southern Highland Handicraft Guild and labeled, according to Jan Davidson in his new introduction to *Mountain Homespun,* as "the coverlet that started the Allanstand Industries."

In Davidson's words, "Before it was a museum piece, it [the coverlet] was used by Frances Goodrich to personify the continuity of her handcraft revival; to raise funds for craft programs, schools, and hospitals; to star in the most dramatic moment of Goodrich's *Mountain Homespun*; and to launch a business that . . . survives to this writing. . . . Before Goodrich got it in 1895, it was a bedspread, probably greatly loved by an old mountain family because one of them made it completely herself. It is a crooked-seam coverlet made about 1850."[8]

The gift of the brown coverlet supposedly inspired Goodrich's work of reviving the weaving industry of Madison County, of building Allanstand into a craft business that became the foundation of the Southern Highland Handicraft Guild's sales success, and of the writing of *Mountain Homespun* and subsequent creation of the legend. Davidson elaborates, "*Mountain Homespun*'s central dramatic incident, the gift of the Double Bowknot, caught the attention of the feature writers, who retold it frequently and compared that gift to the gift of Allanstand [Miss Goodrich donated her business to the guild in 1931] thus making the Guild the final step in conferring the management of mountain handcrafts from the family, to the saintly woman, to a corporation directed by northerners, to a coalition with other production centers."[9]

Well before 1931, though, Berea College's subtle production

and marketing influence had reached Goodrich, who brought Berea's Swedish looms to North Carolina and did away with the "crooked-seam" assembly method.

The crooked seams were both practical (so the coverlet could be taken apart for cold water creek washing) and inevitable; early mountain looms were homemade, cumbersome affairs incapable of the precision weaving demanded by Goodrich and by the northern marketplace. "The irony of the old brown Double Bowknot that started Allanstand—the grand icon of the Appalachian handcraft revival—is that it could not have been sold as an Allanstand coverlet, because, like most old mountain coverlets, it has crooked seams. . . ."[10]

But the old Double Bowknot survives, and dramatic stage interpretations of Frances Goodrich's words from *Mountain Homespun* are used to perpetuate the myth that mothered a modern marketplace.

David Whisnant's scathing description of today's market must be considered:

> Cultural objects, styles, and practices introduced by intervenors sometimes prove remarkably durable, regardless of how little prior basis they had in the culture. The tens of thousands of tourists who visit the publicly funded Folk Art Center at the entrance to the Blue Ridge Parkway or troop through the craft shops of Gatlinburg or Asheville, and the millions who listen to folk-revival musicians on National Public Radio, are "seeing" and "hearing" continuity which is partial at best: they are buying the fruits of hybrid cultures that were long ago severely pruned and grafted. What they have in their shopping bags as they climb back into the station wagons and onto the tour buses is, to use a term familiar to cultural anthropologists, "airport culture."[11]

David Whisnant does not deeply explore whether or not the native mountaineers were *willing* cohorts in the "cultural intervention" of the early twentieth century. I suspect they were, for financial gain.

Some economic truths heavily influenced the early work and established the pattern that still exists, the basic premise of crafts as an economic-development tool.

To succeed in the business world, crafts producers must make what the market will buy. "Bread and butter" production lines pay the bills for the craftspeople who depend upon sales for a livelihood.

Early customers for coverlets from Berea College and Allanstand wanted handcrafted perfection, straight seams, and precise weaving, *done by the quaint and colorful mountaineers whom their purchases were helping to become more civilized.*

The purchase was a dual-purpose action, then, part sentiment and missionary zeal, part insistence upon first-class quality and, as Allen Eaton once suggested, bargain prices.[12] Little, in regards to making what the market wants, has changed.

Like so many other native Appalachians who've learned to perform for pay—the Cherokees who pose in Comanche warbonnets for tourist dollars, the local musicians who learn to play the dulcimer and sing folksongs to have a chance at the contest cash prize, or Garry Barker slipping in and out of the east Kentucky dialect to earn his fee as after-dinner entertainment—the craftspeople have learned to give 'em what they want and laugh all the way to the bank.

The contemporary product most similar to the early coverlets are the quilts, which now sell for three hundred to three thousand dollars each, that seldom if ever are actually used on a working bed.

The traditional everyday Appalachian quilt was a hodgepodge of fabric and color, made to be used, meant to keep people warm in unheated houses.

There were, of course, "show-off" quilts, the "company quilts," fancy and tightly stitched artworks to impress the neighbors and the mother-in-law, and it is these special quilts that are the objects now of the collectors' lust.

The modern marketplace quilts are made of all-new materials, in designer hues, as mass produced as the technique will permit, artful wallhangings meant for the interior designer trade. Machine-pieced quilts are becoming more commonplace and more accepted, and a spin-off industry of printed quilt patterns has evolved to fill the market demand.

It is the reality of the craft world to use technology and shortcuts to lessen the burden of production drudgery—to use electric potters' wheels, bandsaws, and sanders, flyshuttle looms, gas-fired forges, and pneumatic hammers, and even electric carving tools—but the perceived concurrent reality is that customers must continue to believe the myth about quaint mountain craftspeople.

Allen Eaton even subtly endorsed such an approach when he wrote:

> There is, however, no work so good but what some knowledge of the person who is doing it and the attendant circumstances will help make it more significant. . . . To appreciate it [the mountain craft] fully one must know something of the maker, his environment and his opportunities, or lack of opportunities. . . . The deep interest that many people feel in the Highlanders clusters about the true and quaint stories of them which have been captured by social workers, writers, and visitors to the region. To discard this element of appeal would be to throw away what is often a strong bond relating the possessor of an example of Highland handicraft to some mountain character, family, or group of neighbors.[13]

We in the modern Appalachian craft world certainly have not discarded that "element of appeal," even though we have largely discarded the actual crafts and the "true and quaint" lifestyle of which Eaton wrote.

Today in the newly renovated Allanstand gallery in the Southern Highland Folk Art Center, you'll find little or no "folk" art. You'll find today's derivatives of the early crafts—nonfunctional baskets, art pottery, decorator quilts, brooms that can't be used for sweeping, and cornshuck sculptures—plus the highly contemporary glass, wood, fiber, and clay done by the skilled craftspeople who've moved to Appalachia to take advantage of the ready marketplace.

You'll also find the work of the hundreds of Appalachian craftspeople who carefully maintain and perpetuate the "quaint" image and prefer that the buying public never becomes aware that they (the quaint craftspeople) drive eighteen-thousand-dollar vans, live in brick three-bedroom homes, watch cable television, and drink bottled water.

We all *are* willing participants in the marketing myth of quaint Appalachia, perfectly willing to swap image for cash-in-hand.

Sometimes a perceptive observer can see the situation more clearly than can those of us whose daily lives are entwined to the marketplace, and Jim Wayne Miller perhaps did it best with his poem "The Brier Losing Touch with His Traditions."

> Once he was a chairmaker.
> People up north discovered him.
> They said he was "an authentic mountain craftsman."
> People came and made pictures of him working,
> wrote him up in the newspapers.
> He got famous.
> Got a lot of orders for his chairs.
>
> When he moved up to Cincinnati
> so he could be closer to his market
> (besides, a lot of his people lived there now)
> he found out he was a Brier.
>
> And when customers found out
> he was using an electric lathe and power drill
> just to keep up with all the orders,
> they said he was losing touch with his traditions.
> His orders fell off something awful.
> He figured it had been a bad mistake
> to let the magazine people take those pictures
> of him with his power tools, clean-shaven,
> wearing a flowered sports shirt and drip-dry pants.
>
> So he moved back down to east Kentucky.
> Had himself a brochure printed up
> with a picture of him using his hand lathe.
> Then when folks would come from the magazines,
> he'd get rid of them before suppertime
> so he could put on his shoes, his flowered sport shirt
> and double-knit pants, and open a can of beer
> and watch the six-thirty news on tv
> out of New York and Washington.
>
> He had to have some time to be himself.[14]

Part 3

Laughing

Humor Is as Humor Does

I cannot deny the influence of Jim Wayne Miller on my own feeble efforts at free verse. Jim's cleverly worded poetry is even better when *he* does the reading; I seldom miss an opportunity to hear him perform.

Or, without meaning to, to somewhat emulate his approach, to allow laughter to be a part of serious writing.

My first attempt along those lines was "Four Eyes," written the morning after I was fitted with my first pair of bifocal eyeglass.

On the playground of the Goddard School
We taunted Frannie Whitt
Sent her hiding to the outhouse
In tears behind thick glasses.
We called her "four eyes."

Arrogant with perfect vision,
Sharpshooter with rifle or basketball,
Unsmudged by corrective ugliness,
I flaunted 20-20 eyesight,
Hid my college roommate's lenses
And laughed as he blundered,
Searching blind.

Then it happened to me.
Myopia. Astigmatism.
Tiny bookworm lenses
In tortoise shell frames
That slid down my nose when I sweated.

Four eyes.
Forever doomed.
Sore ears. Sore nose. Dirty lenses.
Bent frames, broken hinges.
Fog and frost.

Couldn't swim anymore.
Couldn't shoot pool.
Couldn't wear contact lenses.
Four eyed agony
Made worse by memory.

Twenty years pass.
Fashion and technology attack the issue,
Invent lightweight, designer-signed frames,
Plastic lenses, and sexy advertisements
To prove that men do make passes at girls who wear glasses.
And vice versa, thanks to Woody Allen.

I adjust, accept,
Wear bulletproof two ounce glasses
Designed in Italy
And manufactured
By NASA, I think.

Then the unthinkable, unacceptable
Comes to pass.
Over forty, pre-senile, unbelieving,
I can no longer read my watch
Or anything else close to me.

Bifocals.
Funny little thumbprint smudges
On both lenses.
Tilted head, in the wrong direction,
Can't focus on my toes.

Little Frannie Whitt outgrew her thick glasses,
Got a Ph.D.
And teaches lit at the university.
I saw her last week.
Frannie looked me over, grinned.
And called me "Six eyes."[1]

Another personal favorite was impish Cratis Williams, the east Kentucky native who pioneered the Appalachian studies movement, who could talk to another native for five minutes and pinpoint your origins down to the specific creek, holler, and branch of the family. In 1984, I listened to Cratis speak in Morehead, and that night he told about how his Uncle John reacted to a rare steak served at Green's Restaurant in nearby Salt Lick.

Cratis was obviously still on my mind when, later that year, I spent a week on a Florida beach, fully equipped with notebooks and pens and good intentions of getting some serious work done.

Instead, all I came home with was this three-part, tongue-in-cheek saga of two elderly Kentuckians entitled "At the Beach."

Part One

Lem and Effie
Perched on a wooden bench
To watch seagulls
Line up in a neat row
Ride the swell
And duck their heads underwater to feed
Thirty yards offshore.

"Are them things eating supper, you reckon?"
Asked Lem.
"Or just what are they up to?"
He cut a chew and pondered.

Effie just smiled
And pulled her afghan tighter
Across frail shoulders
To ward off the ocean chill.

"Why, Lem," she said softly,
"Don't they remind you of home
And Caney Creek on a April Sunday?"
Effie clicked her loose lower plate
And watched the gulls duck and float.

"What it is," She finally said,
"Is a baptizing."
Lem studied on that,
Spat a streak of brown ambeer
And almost got a red-bellied lizard.

"Could be you're right,"
Lem finally said.
"But in this here place
A body don't have to duck a girl under water
To see what she's got."

Part Two

"Biggest dadgummed crawdead I ever seen,"
Grunted Lem as the waitress
Made the grand presentation
Of a boiled whole red lobster
And a set of little wrenches.

"Comes with its own tools,"
Observed Lem. "Am I supposed to eat it
Or do a valve job?"
Lem grinned and dug in his pocket.

"Take all that hardware back to the kitchen, honey,"
Lem told the waitress.
He snapped open the long blade
Of his old bone-handled Case.
"I brung my own."

As he cracked shells and ate, Lem told the tale
Of how his Uncle John went over for a Saturday night supper
At Green's Restaurant in Salt Lick
And ordered a fried steak.

"John cut into that meat," grinned Lem
As he chewed on buttery lobster,
"And blood, it run out all over the plate.
Uncle John shoved it back, reared up,
Took out his old Navy .32 calibre,
And shot a hole right through that steak,
The plate, the table,
And the floor."

Lem chuckled.
"Miss Green," he continued,
"Come a running.
'Why'd you do that?'
She squalled.
Uncle John blowed away the smoke,
And looked Miss Green right in the eye.
'I've done killed it,' he said real quiet.
'Now, you take it back and finish cooking it.'"

Lem wiped off his blade
Belched
And grinned.
"Not too bad," he allowed,
"But this here crawdead would taste some better
Fried in a iron skillet
With a little side meat."

Part Three

"Why, them women is near naked,"
Gasped Effie at Neptune Beach.

"Ain't that the gospel?"
Lem agreed happily.

"Look at that one over yonder,"
Hissed Effie.
"Why, a body can see her stretch marks,
And her belly button, and . . ."
Effie blushed.
"Lordy, would you look at where she's gone and shaved herself?"

Lem smiled
And adjusted his new wraparound sunglasses
Settled back in his beach chair
And gave silent thanks
That farsightedness
Runs in the family.[2]

Head of the Holler

Both "Four Eyes" and "At the Beach" are part of the poetry chapbook *Bitter Creek Breakdown,* which brought *Louisville Courier-Journal* columnist Byron Crawford to Berea. During the session, Byron—who earlier had interviewed me for a story on the Berea College "Skittles" game—expressed his pleasant surprise at discovering a good old boy beneath the marketing professional veneer.

"You ought to write a humor column," Byron suggested. "Rural humor."

I was flattered but didn't really pay much attention, but I perked up when Tom Watson called a week or so later. Tom, who worked as a state wire service editor to finance his eclectic monthly newspaper *The Salt River Arcadian,* closed in 1993, asked me to write a column for his "Folklore and Funnies" page.

He'd been referred to me by Byron Crawford.

I agreed to give it a try.

Obviously, with me doing the writing, the slant would be rural and Appalachian, but that wasn't a condition of the request. I agreed, and spent a month laboring over the opening effort. Tom provided the name. To me, "Head of the Holler" is more a state of mind than a geographical location, and I attempted to define that unique point of view in the first column.

I was a hillbilly for the first twenty years of my life, before somebody told me I really was an "Appala chian," then along came the word "redneck" and that seemed to fit, too, so for a long time I've been confused as to which one I really am. I reckon I must be all three: I started out at Gimlet, on Mauk Ridge in Elliott County, then lived at Bluebank and Bald Hill in Fleming County, then went off to Berea College to learn all about dulcimers and Irish folk songs, but spent my summers digging ditches, drinking bootleg Falls City beer, chopping weeds out of the tobacco, and driving a big flatbed truck.

For a Shakespeare class I once wrote a paper that compared Falstaff to one of the good old boys at Nate's Poolroom in Flemingsburg, and then I almost got to leave school because I couldn't say "dead" in one syllable.

Take an eastern Kentucky accent, some Bald Hill backwardness, and a redneck stubborn attitude, and stick all that into a classroom with a Boston proper speech professor, and you get trouble. But I didn't know that the first time I ever had to read in front of the class. I don't remember what I was reading, but somewhere in it, unfortunately, was the word "dead." I must have pronounced it "day-ed."

The professor stopped me. "That word is one syllable, Mr. Barker."

I shrugged. "I know. Day-ed."

"One syllable!" she snapped.

"Okay," I said, not understanding what the problem really was. "Day-ed."

She stopped everything, then and there. "No educated person," she said stiffly, "talks like you do."

"Ever hear of a feller named Lyndon B. Johnson?" I asked.

By now I'm plenty nervous, flustered, embarrassed, and sort of blind stubborn mad.

"Say 'dead' in one syllable," she ordered.

"I'm a doin'," I protested emphatically, "the damned best I know how to do."

She turned white through six layers of pancake makeup.

"Out!" she ordered, trembling finger pointed at the exit door.

I left. The Dean of Men's office was just upstairs, and I figured it was better to surrender than be sent for, so I went on up and told him all that had happened. He was grinning until I got to the very end, then he sort of winced, and I knew I was in deep stuff.

The Dean sort of meditated for a while, then finally said "Go apologize."

"No way," I said. "That old woman made fun of me, right in front of everbody, and I ain't about to go back down there and beg."

He shrugged. "Do you want to finish college?"

I allowed as how I did.

He grinned. "I just told you what you have to do."

Two days later I did it. I bit my lip, swallowed my pride, apologized and begged, and got to stay in school. But I learned me a lesson. Don't cut off your nose to spite your face. Don't spit in the wind. Don't fight with a speech professor who hands out grades. Tell 'em what they want to hear. Don't read out loud anything with the word "dead" in it.

College did and didn't take on me. I came out after four years with a signed, certified, legal degree, the first one ever in my family, and I learned how to pass myself off as a middle-class sort-of-yuppie. It's worked now for over twenty-five years. When I need to I can look, act, and sound like a fairly civilized southerner.

But . . . scratch deep enough, push hard enough, and you'll uncover a hillbilly. A pure redneck. A sort of natural man, one who'd just as soon fight as reason, who'd rather drink beer as white wine, who'd sooner eat pork chops as sushi. I like sleepy old coon hounds, pickup trucks, Willie and Waylon, sweaty long-billed caps, *Hee Haw,* and *The Beverly Hillbillies.* I don't like Japanese cars, cocktail parties, neckties, or sandwiches with the crust chopped off.

Now, I do like running water, heat that comes up through the floor instead of off a Warm Morning stove, a bathroom in the house, air conditioning, and the automatic washer. I've got a computer, a CD player, an Oldsmobile, a pair of pleated Christian Dior britches, a microwave, and a twenty-dollar Rolex watch from New York City.

But, for the life of me, I still can't say "dead" in one damned syllable.[3]

Though I've always loved humor, rural or otherwise, and have had Loyal Jones just across the driveway as an inspiration, I simply could not whip off quick material guaranteed to tickle the funny bone.

So "Head of the Holler" has never been the belly-laugh, thigh-slapping brand of humor I first tried to write.

Obviously I come from a story-telling tradition, the store-porch, potbellied-stove world where humor is used as often to make a serious point as it is to entertain, where laughter is often chosen over tears as the way to deal with difficulty.

I laugh best when I laugh at myself.

That approach also cuts down on lawsuits, fistfights, and gunshots from the darkness.

I like humor that pokes fun at my pretensions, my fancies and foibles, my ego and illusions.

And at yours.

I grew up in a family that had fun. Lots of laughing, teasing, and tale telling were part of every family gathering, every meal, every long workday.

Practical jokes were part of it all; when my father tore down the engine in his first car, a younger brother slipped a handful of bolts and washers into the parts pile. And stayed to watch as Daddy frantically tried to figure why he had so many pieces left over.

The fun could be almost cruel. An uncle abandoned me under the cliffs of Caney Creck to scc what would happen; he learned that even as a ten year old I already knew lots of cuss words (and the way home, fortunately). Live and/or dead snakes were tossed on me, my shoes were nailed to the floor, I found squirrels under my sheets.

But I guess I gave about as good as I got.

The rowdy humor was sort of a lcftover from the frontier days, and the love of fun and laughter seemed to run in families. Some branches—and I suspect rigid religious beliefs were the major influence—seemed to look upon laughter and play as instruments of thc dcvil himself.

Our pranks were often met with gloomy disapproval, stern warnings, the parable of the grasshopper and the ant, and admonitions to grow up and leave our childish ways forever behind.

Thankfully, I never managed to grow up.

For me, "Head of the Holler" is a welcome release, a happy change of pace from the days when I begin to take myself too seriously, and a forum where I can camouflage a few strong statements in the maze of cornball humor.

I'm not a great after-dinner speaker—a stand-up comedian with a polished presentation—and I'm also not a traditional storyteller in the newly popular vein.

I sort of go my own way, though surely influenced by humorists from Mark Twain and Will Rogers to Erma Bombeck and Lewis Grizzard, and every now and then I might stumble into something truly funny.

Much of my humor grows from the not-so-rare position of country boy gone to town, from poking fun at my own past and present efforts to find my way.

Since March 1990, "Head of the Holler" has scrambled off madly in all directions.

Sometimes it's the cornball "rube," remembering his trip to New York City; sometimes it's a frazzled administrator/writer dealing with a domestic crisis, a flooded basement, or a clogged sewer line. Sometimes it's a bittersweet memory of the way things once were.

Always, "Head of the Holler" is one man's jaundiced view of the world he's trying to figure out and function within.

Since November 1991, the column has also been a twice-a-week feature in *The Richmond Register,* and there's even a book of collected columns on the way.

What follows is a cross section, a random sampling of life at the "Head of the Holler," a look at what passes for a reason to laugh in my little corner of the world.[4]

Snake Encounters Make You Wish You Had a Pet Mongoose

Since my novel *Copperhead Summer,* opening with a snake-handling scene in a Tennessee backwoods church, was published in 1985 by Kentucke Imprints, readers have assumed I knew what I was talking about, so they send me news clippings. About the Kentucky preacher whose rattlesnake bit him, so the preacher promptly drank him down some arsenic. Or the New England subdivision built at the foot of a rocky hillside, the winter home to thousands of big rattlesnakes who migrate twice a year across the manicured lawns and blacktopped streets.

The most recent clipping was about copperhead poachers along the Blue Ridge Parkway. Seems a copperhead pelt makes a prized wallet or belt. Me? I wouldn't arrest those poachers. I'd give 'em a bonus.

Because I don't like snakes.

When readers ask me to tell them about my research on snake-handling churches, I give 'em Andy Griffith's old tale about the visitor to the little country church who was trapped in a corner when they started passing out the rattlesnakes. "Where's the back door?" he asked.

"There ain't none," he was told.

"In that case," pondered the visitor, "where do you want one?"

I did my snake-handling research in my living room, rocked back with a copy of John Day's *Bloody Ground* (first published in 1941, reprinted by the University Press of Kentucky in 1981). Mr. Day's description is sufficiently vivid, and the chapter is appropriately titled "Mountain Voodoo." And that's as close as I ever intend to get again to a live copperhead.

I grew up on snake stories, on hoop snakes and blue racers and milk snakes, on how to use a long-handled hoe to chop up serpents who stray too close. My daddy tells about one of my young uncles who learned the hard way to tell the difference between a copperhead and a blacksnake. It seems that a favorite game, in 1930s Elliott County, was to grab snakes by their tails and crack them like a whip to break their necks. The unsuspecting victims would lie on mountain paths at night, drawn by the warmth of the hard, sun-baked ground, and the boys would dispatch them as they walked home from an evening of playing poker and sipping moonshine in somebody's barn.

My uncle, about thirteen at the time, couldn't wait to whip-crack a snake. He finally got to, but he grabbed the tail of about a four-foot copperhead and wrapped it around his head and shoulders. The snake was obviously more surprised than my uncle, so there's no tragic end to the story.

A few years back, a family of garter snakes took up residence in our backyard, in the rocks where there used to be a fish pond. At first my wife had me kill them. Then, she bravely decided to befriend the serpents, so she forbade any further axe murders. I made a deal: I wouldn't go where the snakes were if they wouldn't come where I was.

It worked out pretty good that first summer.

Then, early one dusky spring Saturday afternoon, I came stumbling sleepily into the kitchen and absently stooped over to pick what appeared to be a little piece of wire or rope up off of the floor.

That rope wiggled loose and stuck its tongue out at me.

Back then, I didn't keep an axe or hoe in the kitchen. But one room away was a fireplace and a poker, so in about thirty seconds we had war. I knocked big dents into the linoleum, whacked scrapes into the baseboards, and splattered snake all over the ceiling. When it was over, when my blood pressure dropped to about three hundred and my breathing slowed down to about where it would have been after a four-mile run, I checked out the damages.

My opponent was—or had been—about a foot-and-a-half long, a young garter snake checking out the territory, and for almost a full second I felt real guilty about what I'd done. But, then, I figured, a deal's a deal. The snake should've stayed outside.

Either the rest of the garter snakes were watching, or the cats ate 'em, but pretty soon our rock pile was serpent-free. I hope it stays that way.

If it don't, I've always sort of wanted me a mongoose. Or a WW II flamethrower.

"Colorado Kool-Aid" Almost Caused Pickup Truck Wreck

I never saw a dulcimer until I came to Berea College, never saw a Danish folk dance or knew about our heritage of hundred-verse English ballads sung in an everlasting monotone. Back home, we did sometimes play "Way Down Yonder in the Paw-Paw Patch" and sing some riddle songs, but not a one of us knew where it all came from.

What we did know about was Hank Williams (Sr.) and Hank Snow, the Carter Family and Tennessee Ernie, dobros and fiddles and foot-stompin' fun. My mountain heritage was much livelier than the quaint version presented by Berea College in 1961; my people laughed, drank, fought, loved, lived, and died at a high-spirited rowdy pace more like *Hee Haw* than like the pious flock of Pa Walton.

We had battery-powered radios to listen to the Grand Ole Opry and the Renfro Valley Sunday Mornin' Gathering, and one of my young uncles once worked for a year building him an electric guitar. I sort of publicly abandoned country music when Elvis and Jerry Lee came along, but almost every night snuck and listened to Wayne Rainy, over WCPO in Cincinnati, playing the hillbilly hits.

I loved the Platters, the New Christy Minstrels, Frankie Laine, and even the Beatles, but it was Skeeter Davis, Tammy Wynette, Ernest Tubb, Johnny Cash, and Bill Monroe who could reach down inside my soul and touch something. I about wrecked my truck, laughing, the first time I heard Johnny Paycheck sing "Colorado Kool-Aid," and I still choke up when Hank sings mournfully about hearing that lonesome whistle blow. Waylon Jennings sings my theme song: "I've always been crazy, but it's kept me from going insane."

The shriek of bagpipes makes my hair stand right straight up. I guess my ancestors were piped into battle, and the same warlike concept would work on me. My idea of a really fine funeral would be "Amazing Grace" on the bagpipes, the reading of James Still's poem "Heritage," Miss Dolly singing "He's Alive," then cold beer for everybody.

Country music isn't all I know and like. We were force-fed classics and the opera at Berea College; my Carter County roommate once got a standing ovation when he was reading from an opera. It's the one that includes the line "he raped the daughter and skewered the father," and you can imagine for yourself just how Cyrus, in his hill-country twang, pronounced "skewered."

I never learned to read music, or to identify all the instruments, but sometimes I love a half day of the classics. I like Broadway tunes, too, and I love gospel, blues, and even some jazz.

Closer to home, I prefer Jean Ritchie and the Kentucky Headhunters, Ricky Skaggs and Tom T. Hall, Loretta Lynn and Exile. I love the fiddle, banjo, and mandolin, those instruments of the devil so dearly hated by the early mountain missionary women.

We celebrate old-timey music here in Berea every October, a three-day festival kept pure and honest by Loyal Jones, an often overdue recognition of the real thing.

I watch *Hee Haw* most Saturday nights. And reruns of *The Beverly Hillbillies.* Who among us can't appreciate Granny's references to the "cement pond" or Jed and Jethro's gun-toting expeditions to the country club to "shoot golfs"? If we can't laugh at ourselves, who can we laugh at?

Lots of us aren't the least bit ashamed of our recent mountain heritage, the music and the humor, the old cars and the washing machine on the front porch, the TV satellite dishes and mobile homes.

I am who I am. Half hillbilly, half yuppie, half intellectual, half redneck activist. I know that's too many halves, but I'm also half grandpa and half jock.

Like Waylon says, it's kept me from going insane.

My Kind of Hero: John Updike's "Rabbit" Died

No, the famous novelist isn't expecting. But Harry "Rabbit" Angstrom, my favorite fictional character for several decades, is finished.

Rabbit lived a busy life. In *Rabbit, Run, Rabbit Redux, Rabbit Is Rich,* and *Rabbit at Rest,* well-intentioned Harry Angstrom bumbled along with a changing American society, his "mutt" of a wife, Janice, his inept son, Nelson, financial ups and downs, and—always—his simplistic view of life as defined by once being a small-time high school basketball hero.

In many ways, Rabbit Angstrom was a jerk. But there was something about the guy you had to like and admire, something basically good that kept popping up despite his basic efforts to be evil. I even like the way he died. Rabbit came home from the hospital after a heart catheterization, and that very night slept with his redheaded daughter-in-law. Who confessed. Harry did what he always did. He ran. This time to a Florida condo and eventually to a playground basketball game. The fat old white man earned the black ghetto youngster's respect, but on his winning basket Rabbit sort of fell dead right on top of the kid.

Rabbit went out as the ordinary man's hero, an unlikely winner who never really lost his faith in good things. You have to figure that his daughter-in-law and his granddaughter will miss him, and so will I.

But I tend to favor the heroes—real and fictional—who aren't exactly perfect.

Nobody is, really, but we usually cling to the fiction that the rich, famous, and powerful aren't human, even when the media go all out to discredit our heroes.

Now we know that FDR, Ike, and JFK had girlfriends. Magic has the HIV virus. Pete Rose gambles. Wilt the Stilt has slept with twenty thousand women and is still counting. Daniel Boone didn't really look like Fess Parker. We don't even dare mention Rock Hudson.

Abe Lincoln was maybe a schizophrenic, and they still accuse U. S. Grant of drinking too much. Which mattered not at all to Lincoln: when someone came to complain that General Grant was a drunkard, Honest Abe grinned and suggested that they send a supply of the same brand Grant drank to all the other Union generals.

Richard Nixon has outlived Watergate.

But Jimmy Carter still hasn't lived down his flailing attack on the wet rabbit.

Gerald Ford is best remembered for his bumbling and stumbling.

And I forget who the other guy was, the old movie actor who slept though all the meetings during his eight years in the White House. All things considered, I doubt that Nancy had many opportunities to just say "no."

How long will we remember "Stormin' Norman," the pudgy hero who masterminded the tidy little war we've already forgotten?

Odds are, a hundred years from now, George Custer will be the better known of the two generals. Custer's flaws made him a lot more interesting, more like a fictional hero. And how could you really get into remembering "Schwartzkopf's Last Stand?"

Yellow hair, a wild streak, opponents who hated and respected him, and a dramatic failure assure that Custer's final battle will last much longer in America's folklore than will the gadget war fought over gasoline.

But I hope Kevin Costner never plays Custer in a meaningful movie. Custer surely was never a mumbling robot, and I'd hate to see another legend portrayed nude and void of personality.

There's really no point to all this rambling. It's just that Rabbit Angstrom died, and all this is sort of the way the Rabbit went at thinking about things.

Sort of freed from ordinary logic.

My kind of hero.

Is It a "Tar," a "Tire," or a "Tower"?

Back when I knew it all, when I was nine or ten years old, I righteously corrected the young uncle who was riding home with us to spend a week or two. We were coming back through Morehead, where the college had just built a new water tower, when Uncle Jack spoke up.

"Looky up yonder," he whispered, awed by the huge tank perched on stilts on the mountaintop. "Look at that there water tar."

Superior, better-educated young man-of-the-world that I was, I abruptly corrected my uncle.

"That there ain't no tar," I scoffed pompously. "Tars is what we got on the car. That there thing up yonder is a water tear." I pronounced "tear" as in "rip." Or to go on a tear.

Nobody dared argue with my superior command of the English language. I was, after all, the hotshot young scholar. If I said a "tower" was a "tear," that's exactly what it was.

I did, though, get a rough reprimand from my father for being so righteous, so I pouted the rest of the way home and then hid in the barn with my dog until dark.

A few days later I heard a teacher properly pronounce "tower" and cringed, hoping nobody who'd been in the car was listening. And that may have been the exact moment I decided I'd better stick to writing and leave the spoken word to those better equipped to handle it.

On paper, my words came out just like other people's.

But I was in a forgiving sort of school system, where an English teacher once referred to the Roman soldiers wearing "hemlets," so I ventured to speak out loud again by the time I was about a sophomore in high school.

Public speaking was to cause me the most early grief. I had to work so hard in my effort to speak proper English that I'd forget what it was I was supposed to say or do; one Valentine's Day, in front of the whole faculty and student body, the role-model senior and student council president got rattled and crowned the wrong girl queen.

Somebody hissed a correction from backstage.

I suavely took back the crown.

And made two mortal enemies. The offended, publicly embarrassed girl and her boyfriend. Her very large, very angry boyfriend.

What eventually saved my life was my total humiliation, and the fact that most everybody understood just how nervous a country boy can get on stage.

Later, in college, I drew a speech teacher who lambasted me so often in front of the class that I developed sort of a stubborn immunity to her prejudices against the way I naturally talked. And somewhere along the line I simply quit trying to be like everybody else.

I *did* finally learn to speak fairly standard English, and they tell me my east Kentucky twang has mostly worn off.

I can now pronounce "tower" and "tire." When I want to.

But, sometimes, when I'm really tired (or "tarred") my speech slips right back to where it started out, years ago in Elliott County. My boyhood lisp—from the time I fell head-first into a wheelbarrow full of glass and cut my tongue off (another longer, true story)—returns, I leave all the edges off the words I say, and I realize the people around me are suddenly straining to understand what I'm saying.

That's when I'd *like* to quit and go home, back to where people talk the way they're supposed to, where I don't have to enunciate the "i" or labor over such trivial details as putting a "g" on the end of words.

Loyal Look-Alike

During the Sixteenth Appalachian Studies Conference at East Tennessee State University in Johnson City, Tennessee, Loyal Jones was presented with the first Cratis D. Williams Service Award for his contributions to Appalachian studies.

Loyal, soon to retire after almost twenty-five years as director of Berea College's Appalachian Center, deserves that recognition and much more; he is *the* prominent figure in the study of this region, the best-loved and most in-demand speaker and writer on Appalachian issues.

He's the best-known personality in a world of colorful figures.

That's why I felt a little guilty when, the morning after Loyal had been honored in Tennessee, two different people came up to congratulate *me* for the recognition.

We were all wearing name badges, so both eventually figured out they were off track by about a million accomplishments and went stuttering and blushing off into the crowd searching for the real honoree.

I'm used to it.

I'm mistaken so often for Loyal Jones that it's a standing joke. While, on Sunday morning, I was laughing with Loyal about the most recent confusion, another conference participant came over to stare and ask "Has anybody ever told you two how much you look alike?"

It *is* a one-way confusion, though.

Nobody ever asks Loyal if he's me.

So, fortunately, he never gets blamed for any of the stuff I've done or said.

But we sort of looked each other over, that Sunday morning in Tennessee. Similar size, hair, glasses, and noses. We both like corduroy jackets and comfortable shoes. Our offices in Berea are about thirty yards apart. We both write, one with considerably more success than the other, and we share a love for mountain ways and mountain humor.

We both show up at a lot of the same places.

Loyal is a native of western North Carolina, and for six years I lived and worked close to where he comes from. We know a lot of the same people.

He's one of my longtime heroes.

So, tempted though I may be at times, I don't ever abuse the confused opportunities to pretend to be Loyal Jones.

I'd get caught, anyhow, once my lack of knowledge got exposed.

Only the late Cratis Williams, the Lawrence County, Kentucky, native who pioneered Appalachian studies, was Loyal Jones's equal when it came to knowing, understanding, and appreciating the mountain culture. Cratis had, and Loyal has, a unique ability to both understand everyday Appalachian living and to write and speak with academic clout.

Loyal's more formal studies of the region's music, religion, humor, and literature are strengthened, always, by his "insider's" awareness and love for the sometimes imperfect people who are the backbone of an ageless culture.

Loyal Jones *is* an Appalachian, not just a studied expert on Appalachia. He prefers the real thing to a practiced reproduction. His festivals of music and humor draw on real people, native talent, from living practitioners rather than yellowed archives.

Yet, he is equally at home, equally competent and prominent, in the academic world. He speaks, teaches, and writes with absolute authority (then can chuckle at us and at himself for taking it all so seriously).

So, if people want to confuse me with somebody else, now you can see why I'd just as soon it be Loyal Jones.

And, when they make the movie about Loyal, I'll volunteer to be his stunt double.

The Trauma of Tearing Down a Little Girl's Playhouse

My house is the one that looks like nobody lives here.

Tangled deep grass, overgrown shrubbery, half-finished decks, piles of brush and rotted planking, and gullies washed out down the steep driveway have, I'm sure, irritated the neighbors for the past eleven years.

I have good intentions. It makes sense to do it yourself and save money. And you'd think a feller that grew up clearing new ground, building barns, trucking, digging ditches, and raising burley tobacco could easily keep up with less than a half acre of city hillside.

I could, too, I tell my wife, if I had me a team of mules, a big flatbed truck, a chainsaw, a bushhog, extension ladders, posthole diggers, and two or three full-time helpers.

She allows as how I'd get more done if I didn't sit around reading or writing all the time and if I was at home more than three or four weekends a year.

I don't know. Sometimes I miss my rental years, when all you had to do was call the landlord when stuff needed fixing. And, part of the time, I'm working at a severe handicap; we never had any plumbing when I was growing up, so I never got to learn about faucet washers, leaky pipes, and clogged sewer lines.

But, I also admit, I get distracted easy.

One September Saturday I sat out to tear down my daughter's rotted old playhouse, the one we built up on stilts the summer of '79, the one with hinged windows, a peaked roof, electricity, a yellow door, and outer walls of hand-rived white oak splits.

Beth was about nine years old, a coltish long-legged little girl with missing teeth, an engaging devilish grin, and an imaginary pet snake named Georgie, when we built her miniature chalet on the hillside. Now she's twenty, a junior at the University of Kentucky, and a little amused that I'm reluctant to tear down her old playhouse.

So I finally gathered up hammers, crowbars, leather work gloves, and my old crooked-handled mattock, knocked off the outer shingles, then busted down the locked door to crawl up inside and complete the demolition. But, inside, I found an old faded pink teddy bear, a half-played game of Chinese Checkers, a little box full of old dime-store costume jewelry, and such a flood of memory and emotion that I had to climb blindly back out and go away.

I spent that whole Saturday afternoon writing a poem, "Attractive Hazard," and didn't get back around to finishing up the demolition job until the next April.

Then I ran head-on into another problem. What do you do with, in a city, piles of torn asphalt shingles, rotted plywood, and splintered pine studs? And the load of brush that had to be cut down to get to the playhouse?

The city offered to haul away the brush, no charge. All I had to do, they said, was cut it into two-foot lengths, bundle it, and have it at the curb the one day of the year they pick up. The clerk didn't laugh when I asked if they'd like the limbs gift-wrapped, polished, and pre-weighed.

I allowed as how I'd rather just burn the whole mess. You can't do that, I was informed, anywhere inside the city limits. Or outside, except by special permission.

But they finally did give me a landfill permit, after I showed my driver's license, social security card, Visa, and American Express. And gave the make, model, year, color, and license tag of the truck I'd be using.

So now the back corner of our yard is empty again, except for the big holes the dog dug back in under the playhouse.

But, you know, with a pair of two-year-old grandsons, I might ought to start building again. The boys will need a fortress. And I've got some treated pine posts left over from the deck steps I never did get finished.

The Thanksgiving Feast, Interrupted by a Critter

Thanksgiving Day, in rural Kentucky, is a time to eat, butcher hogs, and go hunting. Last year, we didn't butcher hogs.

But we ate and sort of hunted.

We live smack-dab in the middle of Berea, a sort-of-city

about ten thousand people strong, but in an older section near the railroad tracks and with an abandoned city alley running through the backyard. The alley means we have animals. Possums, squirrels, rabbits, some snakes, and maybe other creatures that venture out only at night inhabit the thickets and search out the garbage. My wife feeds the birds, the birds are food for the neighborhood's cats, and nature's cycle goes on. The busy, always hungry squirrels take birdseed, so we use stale bread sometimes in a vain attempt to keep the critters from tearing down the expensive new "squirrel-proof" bird feeder.

Last Thanksgiving, we and our backyard zoo were surprised by cold weather and heavy snowfall, an unexpected onslaught that put unfrozen water and available food at a premium. Our yard was busy, almost frantic, full of squawking, flapping, food-fighting birds, greedy squirrels, and one unwelcome newcomer.

A rat.

Or some type of huge, short-haired rodent. He was feasting alongside the squirrels, doves, blue jays, and grackles, quite at home and pleased with himself, confident and so unafraid he didn't even run when I came outside.

Now, I don't mind the possums. And even the snakes, as long as they stay on their side of the agreed-upon boundary, are okay. But I do draw the line at rats.

By the second day my wife had named the intruder "Willard," and I'm wondering how, in the middle of town, to get rid of an alley rat. Poison might get birds and squirrels, shooting isn't allowed in the city limits, I don't have a hand grenade.

Thanksgiving Day interrupts.

Kids, wives, husbands, mother-in-law, and grandson come for turkey and the trimmings, and in the midst of the preparation bustle somebody looks out the kitchen window. There's Willard the rat, dining greedily on bread and sunflower seed hulls.

My mother-in-law is horrified. What if, she asks, that rat comes in the house and bites the baby?

We have in-kitchen advice from one practicing attorney, one second-year law student, one psychologist, one medical office manager, one retired teacher, one eighteen-month-old boy.

Our son-in-law is of a more practical vein. "My shotgun," he says, "is in the truck."

I decline the honors. Bifocals and a twenty-year absence from shotgun shooting enter into the decision. I might hit a neighbor. Or, worse still, I might miss the rat. But I authorize the execution, and son-in-law goes into action. Booted, vested, loaded shotgun at the ready, he circles and stalks. With a gallery, noses pressed to fogged-over windowpanes.

There's a sudden soft pop, and a blur of flying rat.

It's over.

The birds and squirrels resume feasting. And, shortly, so do we.

Then one son, the bare-bones law student at the elitist University of North Carolina in Chapel Hill, gets the giggles. His classmates already think, he explains, that all Kentuckians are redneck hillbillies. So, he grins, wait until he goes back with this tale, in dialect: "Well, my maw, you know how she slops the critters out back of the homeplace, so's they's birds and possums and sich all over the place, and Thanksgiving Day they was this big old rat that come. Grandma, she was riled up and wanted to take a hoe to the varmint, but my sister's man, he says they's a gun in his pickup truck. So Chuckie, he goes and gets his shotgun out of the cab and sneaks around and blasts that rat to kingdom come. Then we all set down and et our vittles."

The vision of a tarpaper shack propped up on stilts over the creek, slop slung out the back door, a ringer washer on the front porch and a moonshine still up by the outhouse, a tobacco-chewing granny in sunbonnet and brogans, a bib-overalled son-in-law with a battered felt hat, drooling, toting a long-barreled flintlock shotgun, dissolves us all into helpless laughter.

But then, somewhere along the line, we come up with this sobering thought: the preppy, sheltered UNC law students will never realize that the story is being exaggerated.

There Must Be a Law That Requires Grits in the South

I read in this newspaper the other day that if a customer ordered a bagel in a Georgia restaurant they'd bring him a small hound dog.

All things considered, the beagle might make a better breakfast.

Sometimes I have trouble eating in a restaurant south of the Kentucky border too. I hate grits, and to the south of us they come with breakfast whether you want 'em or not. I think it's a Confederate law.

I like hominy. But when they take the same stuff, grind it up, slop it out runny on a plate with a pound of butter melted on it, I lose my appetite for eggs and ham. I finally worked up enough nerve to face down the shocked disbelief of waitresses, and now I ask them to hold the grits. Some do, some don't. It ain't easy to get a waitress to break the law with people watching.

Last summer in South Carolina I ordered unsweetened iced tea. The waitress blinked. "Y'all from up north, hon?" she demanded loudly. Fifty definitely un-northern customers twisted to stare. A hundred eyes glared. Don't try to tell me the Civil War ended in 1865. I drank sweet tea.

To me the real South is swampy north Florida and south Georgia, sticky, hot places where I visualize—waiting just off the interstate, drooling—hordes of alligators, cottonmouth moccasins, and six-foot rattlesnakes, all mad because they have to live there with the heat, little black bugs, and grits. And I keep expecting fat deputy sheriffs in Dodge pickup trucks, just itching to throw me up against a fender and growl, "You in a heap of trouble now, boy."

Probably, the tourists who pass through Kentucky on I-75 harbor similar fears and misconceptions. They expect the Dukes of Hazzard to come charging out in an orange NASCAR racer, expect a Hatfields and McCoys feud to break out across the highway (the last McCoy I talked to, by the way, was lugging around a cookbook of family recipes instead of a .30-.30 Winchester carbine).

Some outsiders don't even like country ham. That's blasphemy, but it happens. One of my wife's cousins married a girl from the Northeast, and when she came to visit, the new mother-in-law went all out, really put on the dog, bought a home-cured ham, and boiled and baked it to perfection. The daughter-in-law kind of worried the meat but didn't eat it; she confessed, weeks later, that she thought she'd married into a family of morons who ate rotted meat.

I love country ham so much that for twenty-five years I've rearranged travel schedules so I'd wind up in Bean Station, Tennessee, at mealtime. I don't order beans at the Harris Court Restaurant; I order and enjoy the best restaurant ham in the world. When I first stopped there, in 1965, you could get three biscuits with ham for a dollar, complete with redeye gravy (what Grandma called "sop" because you used a biscuit to sop it up). The prices have gone up just a little, but the ham's as good as ever. And, yes, they serve grits with breakfast.

I grew up one of nine kids where we got homemade biscuits every morning and a big pan of crispy cornbread with every dinner and supper (dinner's at noon, supper's at suppertime at our house). My mother had to feed eleven people on next to nothing, and she did, and I'd still risk bodily harm for the crispy corners off a pan of her cornbread.

The odd number of us caused problems when we had pie. There's no way to slice two pies into eleven equal pieces. War broke out to see who'd get the extra slice, and I don't ever remember winning.

But I got even with my brothers and sisters. I took a job mowing, with teams of horses, for a neighbor. Every day, at dinnertime, his wife would bake a whole pie and we'd split it down the middle. I got half; he got half.

And on top of that, he paid me two dollars a day.

The Snaphook System Has Revolutionized Cap Wearing

A few faculty members at the college where I work sometimes try to fit into the local culture by showing up downtown in jeans, boots, and long-billed cap.

They do try, and for that I'll give them credit. But usually the glossy new boots are from L. L. Bean, the jeans are stiff and awkward, and the cap—the crowning glory—is unsweated, flat-billed, and about as out-of-place as sweat pants at the opera house.

Not everybody knows how to wear a cap. It's something you're sort of born and raised into, that's learned early and for practical reasons. A good, broke-in cap is sun visor, sweatband, and bee swatter, intimate protection against sun, wind, tobacco gum, grease, dirt, and waspers; these days it's also an ornament and walking billboard, a way to advertise, offend, or entertain.

I don't know who invented the cap. Certainly baseball made them more popular, and then manufacturers discovered we'd actually pay cash money to wear their commercials. Whoever invented the one-size-fits-all snaphook system revolutionized the marketplace for caps. I remember caps that came in sizes, and I think I wore a 7 3/4, but now none of that matters.

I keep six or eight caps on hand at all times. Two or three are heavy, for wintertime use, and the rest are summer styles in various stages of the use cycle. I always keep a dress cap on hand, a clean new one, for formal occasions such as family reunions, all-day meeting, or supper at the People's Restaurant. And, always, there's at least one cap at the other end of the use cycle: greasy and misshapen, much sweated, battered, and abused, comfortably broken-in and familiar, an old buddy who's shared lots of life and work. I hate to part with a good cap; it's sort of like tossing away one of the kids or a good mongrel dog.

Most of my caps are "in-betweeners," some still being unstiffened and sweated into shape, some ready to wear, others I've given up on wearing but can't bring myself to throw away just yet.

I've never really gone shopping to buy a cap. I'll see one and buy it, or get caught somewhere in the sunshine and have to take whatever I can get (and pay anywhere from five to twenty dollars). Sometimes people give me caps, like the 101st Airborne model my son brought me, and once businesses would hand out caps (and nail aprons) to regular customers. Softball team sponsors always provide caps, but three games into the season mine's so filthy they'd probably rather I wouldn't wear it out in public.

I keep my caps stashed on top of the refrigerator, handy to the back door, though I know cap "collectors" who build or buy ornate display units. Some line a row of caps up across the back window of their car.

But, somehow, you can always spot the one who wears the cap just for effect, who doesn't really understand what a good thing he's got. His bill isn't creased—it's still flat, and clean—and he wears his cap too high, too loose. A cap is meant to be tugged down tight, to mold itself to whatever head it's on, with an often-fingered bill pulled low enough to block out the sun's glare.

There's no science to wearing a cap. It either sort of comes natural or it don't. And I've never yet seen a set of instructions.

Maybe that's why the professors don't ever seem to learn how. There's no book, with footnotes and a bibliography, on "How to Wear a Cap." That'd be a worthy project for a group of sociologists, anthropologists, and folklorists to tackle—with, of course, a large research grant—and I'm sure there's a university press somewhere that would publish the results.

To sort of cap off the effort.

Don't Leave Home without It

Recent surveys that show that eastern Kentucky is the per capita murder capital of the United States shouldn't really come as a surprise.

Nor should three corollary theories: we kill kinfolks, not strangers; shootings increase in direct proportion to the unemployment rate; and we're much more likely to plug the brother-in-law when we're drinking.

A rural Kentucky household without weapons is a rarity. We've got shotguns, deer rifles, .22s for varmints and target practice, heavy-duty handguns for serious work, muzzle loaders, full-automatic assault rifles, Saturday night specials, and probably a few bazookas, flamethrowers, and portable missile launchers.

Stir together more weaponry than you'll find in any small spot in the world (with the possible current exception of Kuwait City), the highest unemployment rate in the United States, and a legal system that looks the other way and the result is lots of stiff bodies.

Holidays also affect the kill rate. Free time and whiskey, depression, and the gathering of the clan create a killing climate, and those who survive Thanksgiving and Christmas should breathe a deep sigh of relief.

Another factor in our number one ranking is that we can flat out shoot straight. Unlike the television cops, crooks, and cowboys, we hit what we shoot at. It sort of comes natural: little boys are handed their rifles almost at birth, and every gathering includes some show-off target shooting. I'm not sure any more just *why* the ability to shoot is so important, but I taught my own son and gave him a rifle (then the U.S. Army honed his skills, handed him an M-16, and shipped him to Saudi Arabia).

My grandfather was killed in an early 1920s Christmas Eve gunfight in Elliott County; he was drunk, celebrating the holiday, using his .32 Smith and Wesson instead of firecrackers. Somebody didn't understand that Granddaddy was just having fun and shot back.

Seventy years later, things haven't changed much. Granddaddy's horse has been replaced by the pickup truck, and the firepower is much more awesome. The .357 magnum or lethal 9 mm automatic does a lot more damage than a little navy issue revolver, and today Granddaddy would be sorely outgunned.

Maybe the good news in all the bad news is that we do tend to kill mostly each other. Tourists, traveling salesmen, and candidates for governor are relatively safe in eastern Kentucky, though antipoverty workers and gun-control advocates would do well to travel only in broad daylight, well escorted. And don't ever, not even indirectly, threaten anybody's life or land. No jury convicts if there's a possibility of self-defense or justifiable homicide (which means, in plain English, that the victim *needed* killing).

So, somebody might someday ask, how do we lower the incidence of violent death in eastern Kentucky?

Damned if I know. Gun-control laws are a farce: we have enough guns and ammo already on hand to last a couple of centuries, and small-arms technology isn't likely to advance so much as to render our firepower obsolete. Tougher law enforcement is unlikely, especially when our state troopers and deputies themselves sometimes indulge in a little off-duty mayhem.

Probably the answer is very similar to the answer to the rest of eastern Kentucky's problems: education, economic development, patience, and prudence. Given enough time, we'll probably all move away or finish murdering each other. But, until then, don't go home for Christmas without your handguns, ammo belt, and flak jacket.

Moonshining Tame Compared to Drugs

When I was in college, two of my friends from Harlan County regularly brought back quart jars of moonshine whenever they'd been home for the weekend.

A quart may not sound like a lot (especially when compared to the Union general during the Civil War who roared, when he discovered his stock of drinking liquor was low, "What's two gallons of whiskey amongst one man?"), but when that quart is 150-proof clear corn whiskey it can do a lot of damage.

Like the Sunday night I'd carried a soft drink back to the dorm room in a paper cup, then left it on my desk when I went to answer a phone call. When I got back, I assumed the clear half-cup of liquid was melted ice. I drank it down in one gulp.

Even my teeth got singed. I felt that moonshine all the way down, red-hot and stinging all the way, and for five minutes or so I couldn't breathe. My eyes watered. My ears burned. My knees went weak.

The paralysis was temporary. In time, I regained my voice. And asked, all trembly and creaky, for another dollop of Kentucky moon.

Moonshine is *not* sipping whiskey, not the stuff you'd put in a little stemmed crystal glass and carry around with your little finger stuck out, not the stuff you'd decorate with an olive or slice of lime. It's raw, crude, and potent, more suited for passing around in the parking lot or out in the barn, the white-hot stuff of legend, folklore, feuds, and fascination.

Unfortunately, it's also the same stuff when made wrong—of a painful death. The distillers who use old car radiators and shortcuts sometimes market pure poison, full of wood alcohol, lye, and Lord knows what else, so the market for Kentucky's illicit lightning is sort of slipping.

The best buyer's rule of thumb is to know who's making the shine, then to personally observe somebody drink the stuff and actually live, with no side effects other than the world's worst hangover.

But it's more than quality control that has killed off the moonshine market. A hundred or so years of relentless prosecution, prison terms, and bashed-up stills have sort of taken the fun out of it, and in most places the legal stuff is cheap and easy to get.

Moonshine runners gave us NASCAR racing, and now the

souped-up cars run flat out on contained tracks, unencumbered by hidden, heavy tanks of illegal whiskey. The classic old movie *Thunder Road* documented the cars, chases, and the culture of the men who outran decades of law officers and made every red-blooded young southern boy yearn for a 1957 Ford with dual exhausts, a four-barrel carb, and a racing cam.

Some Kentuckians still practice the ancient art. As I write, behind me on the shelf is a half-full Mason jar of Rockcastle County moonshine, and there are a handful of reliable suppliers scattered across the state.

Most of the massive law-enforcement effort is now aimed at harder drugs, the much more profitable modern alternative to moonshine, the outlaw culture that thrives for much the same reasons illegal whiskey was once so common.

In a land with little economic activity, double-digit unemployment, and enough rugged hollers, rock houses, and hillsides to conceal any country boy worth his salt for fifty years, it's no surprise. And it has turned ugly: helicopters and drug-sniffing hounds are met with booby traps and snipers; sheriffs and other public officials are being bought off; and some of the innocent victims are mere children.

Somehow, except for being illegal, moonshining was an honorable profession.

That won't ever be said about the drug dealing.

I already know that what I just said sounds two-faced, so you don't have to call or write to berate me.

I don't have any simple answers. I just know that—in much of the mountains—it's no longer safe to go walking through the woods.

And that's just a minor side effect of the real shame.

Although the Fight Was Lost, a Hero for the Day Emerged

I'm a pacifist, up to a point. I'll turn the other cheek until both cheeks are raw and bend over backwards so far my shoulders almost touch the ground. Up to a point.

I don't like pain. I don't like to fight. I don't understand how it can be fun to get your nose busted, eyes blacked, and teeth knocked loose.

But growing up where I did, when I did, a boy didn't have any choice. Sooner or later, you just had to fight. Whether you won or lost was almost immaterial, but somewhere along the line a feller had to prove he'd hit back.

I won some, lost some. I won all the ones I was pushed into, when I'd finally get hurt or get so mad I'd try to kill somebody. When I was in the seventh grade, a new kid in school, I finally pounded one tormentor's face in the gravels down by the outhouse until a teacher could drag me off; that necessary outburst made life bearable on the school ground, proved that the quiet kid who did his homework could also be dangerous.

Daddy wasn't a lot of help. He said don't ever start a fight but don't ever run from one, and a licking at school meant another one at home. He said a scared man is the dangerous one, the one who'll kill you.

I started one fight, my whole life, and that one time I was dumb enough to pick on somebody a foot taller, three years older, a young adult with a punch like a mule's kick.

We used to have "8th Grade Day" in Fleming County, a spring migration of all the county eighth-graders into town for a close-up look at high school. Me, I knew I'd be going there in the fall—my older sister and brother were already high school students—so I was pretty confident and cocky. Had on my only new shirt, my best jeans, and was running over with arrogance and superiority.

Back then, less than half of us from the county schools went on past the eighth grade. One of ours who wasn't going to go was Cletus, who'd taken ten or eleven years to finish the lower grades because he'd missed so many classes to work on the family farm. Cletus was already sixteen, the end of mandatory school in Kentucky, so he was ready to farm full time. That day, Cletus took exception to my eagerness and excitement about high school, and—unfortunately—said something to me in front of a bunch of giggly girls.

Cletus and I went through the ritual, the "Says who?" and "Says me" and a shove or two, then I made my fatal error. I hit Cletus. Not much. Just a little left hook to his belly. Like hitting, I suddenly realized, my heart sinking fast, the trunk of a big oak tree.

Two more punches were thrown. Cletus bent me over with a belly blow, then straightened me up with a roundhouse right to the nose. My big nose. I woke up on the bathroom floor, surrounded by teachers and boys from my class, with about a pint of blood—my blood—spattered all over. I laid there for a minute, to catch my breath and think on just how I could come out of this mess with some dignity intact.

Surely, I reasoned, Cletus wouldn't hit me again with all these people around. So I spit some blood and came thrashing angrily up off the floor. "Where's he at?" I demanded, stumbling and shoving away the many hands that held me. "I'll kill him."

The boys backed off, wide-eyed at my rage, and for a second I was afraid they were actually going to let me go looking for Cletus.

"He left," somebody finally whispered. "Running."

"Big chicken," I grunted through swollen lips. I took a step and staggered, felt for my face and found it, now with a crooked nose. My new shirt was a bloody mess. They led me out into the hallway, and then I saw who'd scared big old Cletus so bad he ran. My favorite teacher, Miss Belle, was mad as a hornet and red as a beet, and the sight of her would have frightened away a pack of starving timber wolves.

"What happened?" Miss Belle demanded.

Before I could figure out a good story the girls chimed in. "Cletus started it," they said. There for a minute, I loved the three little liars with all my heart.

For the rest of that day I was a hero. Little kids ogled, girls gently felt of the bruises, and my buddies muttered darkly about revenge on Cletus.

By losing the fight I'd started, I was a hero. You figure it. But I never look a gift horse in the mouth, so I made the most of the opportunity. By the time we were to get on the bus and go home, the official version of the fight had me risking life and limb (and nose) to protect three helpless, innocent girls.

But Cletus never did come back to school, not even to pick up his diploma.

Maybe that one fight I won by losing is the reason I don't fight anymore.

This Sleeping Dog Had Bite Worse than Bark

When my good old dog Bum had to be put to sleep, I went over to a neighbor's barn to get a new puppy for my baby brother. I didn't pick out the little brown dog Sam; he chose me, growled, and attacked my leg with sharp puppy teeth, then chewed on me all the way to the house.

Jon, who'd grown up with the old dog, swore angrily that he'd never have another pet. Persistent little Sam, who seemed to understand Jon's heartbreak, followed the boy's every move until he won him over.

Sam grew into about a hundred pounds of one-man dog. He adored Jon, protected my mother, tolerated the rest of the family, and hated strangers. Sam did not permit petting, except by a chosen few, and absolutely no one set foot in the yard until Sam granted his permission. And he granted that permission reluctantly, only when ordered to do so by someone in authority.

When Sam was maybe five years old, in his adult prime, some local boys decided to rob my father's shed, to steal the tools and building supplies they knew were stored there.

That shed was also Sam's bedroom. The three intruders met long white fangs, fearsome snarls, and the meanest dog on Mudsock Road. They escaped, leaving behind only some tattered pants legs and fresh blood.

Determined, the three boys figured it out. They'd kill the dog first, then go back to rob the shed. A week later they returned, safe inside a pickup truck, rifle ready.

The rifleman must have been a little unnerved when Sam came out growling, and he pulled his shot. Sam took a .22 slug through the shoulder, a flesh wound, finally allowed the wary vet to treat him, and came home sore, limping, and mad at the world. At dusk, Sam hobbled off to his shed to lick his wound and get some rest.

About midnight, the three locals shut off the truck engine and coasted the last hundred yards up to the shed. They crept out cautiously, waited, and—convinced that they'd killed the big dog—snuck inside the shed.

Sam was surprised, and surely delighted, to recognize three old foes. Stiff, mad, in no mood for forgiveness, Sam came out of the corner chewing.

From the house, Daddy heard blood-curdling screams, crashes, and thuds, and Sam's savage snarls. He grabbed some pants and his old twelve-gauge and went to help Sam.

As if Sam needed any help.

The big dog took out all his pain and frustration on three screaming young thieves, and, just as they broke loose and ran for the truck, my father gave them the first round of Number Six buckshot. Right into the truck. Daddy reloaded, tried to get Sam out of the line of fire, then blasted away again. The taillights, rear window, and most of the rusty paint disappeared from the lumbering pickup.

Sam, sort of disgusted that the human had interfered with his fun, snorted and limped on back to his bed of gunnysacks.

Fantasy Becomes Reality

I finally got to hold a boyhood dream in my hands.

It's a Winchester .30-.30 carbine, the short-barreled trapper's model, the cowboy's saddle rifle from the old western movies and TV shows.

Since I don't do any trapping, don't own a saddle or a horse, haven't been deer hunting in twenty-five years, and hardly ever fire a weapon of any sort, you may wonder why I'd want the trapper's Winchester so badly.

It's sort of the adult descendant of the old Red Ryder BB rifle. A toy. A wall ornament to commemorate the wonder years. A remnant of those childhood days of the old red felt cowboy hat, decorated high-heeled boots, and set of gaudy six-shooters strapped low around the hips of Gene Autry, Roy Rogers, the Cisco Kid, Johnny Mack Brown.

Except that, after a friend finally tracked down the little rifle and delivered it to me, after a couple of hours of handling and admiring the precision and beauty of the Winchester, I decided I ought to have some ammunition.

The bullets are about three inches long. Lethal, ugly, and all business. Brass, copper, and lead. Tools for killing.

The packet of ammunition sort of deflated my dream. Drove home some unpleasant reality. A rifle, even my tiny toy of a saddle gun, is for killing.

The M-16A army carbine my son carried to Saudi Arabia and back was a much uglier, much lighter, much more efficient weapon. Virtually indestructible and sort of harmless looking, the M-16 can empty a clip in seconds. It's sole, admitted purpose is warfare. It's a necessary element of military action. It's all business. No romance, no movie memories.

A killing machine.

The original lever-action Winchester carbine, or the Sharps version first used during the Civil War, was equally dramatic, or more so, when it was first introduced.

One cavalryman with a repeating rifle could fire seven rounds while an infantryman was trying to reload his cumbersome, conventional cap-and-ball rifle.

That war ended before the full impact of rapid-fire rifles could be felt.

But the repeating rifle and the Colt revolver moved West to become legends, the stuff of books and movies, the tools of the famous and infamous lawmen, outlaws, cavalrymen, and the desperate Native Americans fighting for a lost cause.

That's where, about seventy-five years later, I came along. The old cowboy movies, the comic books, and then the TV shows romanticized an ugly period of American history and transformed the Colt .45 and Winchester .30-.30 into living legends.

Made me want the little saddle rifle so badly I still had to have it, about forty years after I'd put aside the boyish games.

I love my little carbine.

It'll live happily, on display, and be handed down someday to a grandson.

I put the cartridges away so I wouldn't have to see them, wouldn't have to visualize what just one of them could do to a living creature.

Like so many childhood fancies, the real things isn't exactly what I expected. It *has* helped remind me of the differences between fiction and reality.

I'll keep the Winchester as a reminder of both.

Of wonderful memories, of brutal potential reality.

Another boyhood fantasy turned into adult reality.

Public Speaking Never Gets Easier

Because of my writing and my work, I do a lot of interviews, television, and public speaking. After about thirty years it's easier, almost routine, but that wasn't always so.

Nerves, shyness, my eastern Kentucky accent and dialect, and a demanding speech professor almost ended my college career when I was a sophomore, and my voice isn't nearly as big as I am.

A second speech professor helped some. To start with, she didn't insist that I lose my accent, and then she sort of convinced me that, when I knew what I was talking about, I did a halfway decent job in front of a crowd.

Which was nice, I figured, but not necessary. I had no intention, ever, after graduation, of getting up in front of a crowd and opening my mouth.

Which was true for almost the first two weeks of my first job.

Then my boss casually informed me, late one afternoon, that I'd have to fill in for him the next day as a luncheon speaker. At Asheville's Grove Park Inn, to almost a thousand churchwomen in town for a convention.

I didn't sleep at all that night.

The next morning, baggy-eyed and anxious, I drove up to the Grove Park in my old Falcon, blue oil smoke trailing across the mountainside, me in a nine-dollar plaid jacket and white socks, my only tie knotted over the bigger knot in my throat.

The doorman finally let me go inside, and when I saw what was in there I almost left. In the lobby of the Grove Park, Asheville's historic resort to the Vanderbilts, Fords, Hemingways, and Fitzgeralds, the fireplaces are bigger than my house. The lobby itself would hold a football game. Everywhere, lushness and wealthy gentility prevail. Nobody else is wearing white socks.

In the banquet room, the speakers table is elevated. There really *are* a thousand women seated in the room. The waiter brings a fruit salad platter bigger than my spare tire.

If this is salad, I'm thinking, what's the main course? I sort of nibble, to save room for the entree, but when it's too late figure out that the salad *was* lunch.

It's time for me to talk. The introduction is short. I don't have a title. All I've ever done is graduate from Berea College on a rainy Sunday night two weeks earlier.

I rediscover that day what is still true: it's easier to speak to a huge audience of total strangers, protected by a podium and dimmed lights, than it is to speak to a small gathering of people you know.

Try as I may, I can't stretch the reading of the Southern Highland Handicraft Guild brochure out for more than ten minutes. But the magic of Berea College saves me. Instead of asking questions about Appalachian crafts, which I could not have answered, they ask me about Berea.

I was too relieved to be scared.

When it was over, I fled, shucked the tie and jacket, put a quart of oil in the Falcon, and rolled happily down off Beaucatcher Mountain.

I stopped for a greasy grilled steak sandwich.

To this day, I'd rather eat *after* the speech. The last thing my nervous stomach needs, just prior to a public appearance, is dry roast beef and instant mashed potatoes.

I'm not really being rude when, today, I just sort of shove the dinner around in the plate when I'm the after-dinner speaker.

I just don't want to throw up in front of two hundred people.

Possumcats on the Prowl

Somebody came in the other day to warn me I shouldn't go hiking in the woods without a weapon.

I thought he was referring to the marijuana farmers, with their booby traps and automatic rifles, but it seems there's a new menace waiting out there.

"Coy-dogs." Half coyote, half domestic dog, this new breed of pups probably does not qualify for American Kennel Club registration. And, word is, they're totally unafraid of humans and more likely to attack than to tuck their tails and run.

If we have any coy-dogs in the alley behind our house I haven't seen them yet, but I wouldn't be surprised to get up some morning and find a pack of them gathered at the back door waiting for a handout.

Everything else does.

Birds, squirrels, cats, rats, and possums visit us daily to squabble over the birdseed, corn, and stale bread.

Something comes out only at night and creates pure bedlam, growling and squalling, thumping across the deck and sometimes the rooftop. I've suspected we have a bobcat or a Tasmanian devil, but now I have a new theory as to what it is that goes bump in the dark.

If dogs and coyotes can mate and produce brainy, fearless, agile offspring, what would you get if you crossed a possum with an alley cat?

Whatever it was, it'd be yellow with stripes, pure hell on garbage cans, and impossible to ever get rid of.

A cunning possum?

Conventional city possums are certainly survivors, but I suspect that has more to do with reproduction rates and the fact that few predators would stoop so low as to eat possum meat.

For years, we kept a huge Dalmatian chained in one corner of our backyard. The good-hearted old dog was hostile only toward mail carriers (after one of them sprayed her with Mace), and all sorts of wild creatures were free to roam safely through the Dalmatian's territory.

Even possums.

Until they tried to come inside her shed and eat her food.

The first possum fatality I wrote off to a good try. The possum saw some food and tried to take it. He died. You'd figure, though, that all the other possums would hear about what happened and stay clear of the huge white dog.

They didn't.

About twice a week, a new possum would lumber into the shed, reach for a mouthful of dog food, and get crushed in sleepy but powerful jaws.

So you can sort of see why I don't rank possums up there with pigs in the animal brain-power comparisons.

But crossbreeding with tough old ragged-eared alley cats could add new dimensions to the possum family.

Like speed. Leaping ability. Wailing. Audacity. A tail that twitches.

The possibilities (or possumibilities) are scary.

A yellow-striped possum that fakes friendliness and rubs up against your legs?

A rat-tailed alley cat that humps up and hisses?

No garbage would ever be safe from a possumcat. Combine the regular possum's glum determination with an old tomcat's innovative and ingratiating personality, and you'd get the world's most perfect, most obnoxious survivor.

It's probably too late to stop it.

I think the crossbreeding has already begun.

So far, the new creatures come out only at night to scavenge, fight, howl, and reproduce.

So far they have not—to my knowledge—attacked humans.

But it's just a matter of time.

Because a possum will eat anything, and cats have been patiently waiting since time began to drop their feline pretense and eliminate the human race.

Gimpy Knees, Gray Hair, No More Basketball

About two years ago I finally quit playing basketball.

Thirty years too late, some would say.

But the noontime game in Berea College's Seabury Gym was hard to give up. Since 1970, I've played volleyball and basketball, even some softball, with Berea faculty and staff, alumni, students, and many others who simply played for the love of sport, exercise, and competition.

The basketball game—with players ranging from under twenty to over fifty, from former college stars to absolute beginners—was (and still is) a self-refereed, physical, hard-fought, and surprisingly skilled shirts-and-skins substitute for lunch.

Some days the gimpy knees, gray hair, and pungent aroma of muscle rubs gave the game a slightly different interpretation—a little slower, a little closer to the floor—and the array of orthopedic braces and eye gear reflected both modern technology and old-fashioned determination. Lots of tape, elastic bandages, and reconstructive surgery can keep a battered basketball player going well beyond his allotted years.

Some aspects of basketball actually improve with the years. When the ability to simply outrun and out-jump the opposition is gone, learning how to play makes a lot more sense. Teamwork gets more important when one-on-one playground moves are something you remember instead of something you instinctively do.

When there are no fans or cheerleaders to impress, no newspaper reporters checking the box scores, individual glory sort of goes to the sidelines and a good pass feels as good as a basket.

Of course, for some us, nothing else ever feels as good, as absolutely right, as a soft, arched jump shot, motions practiced and repeated from childhood to middle age, the celebrated "string music" of sportscaster Joe Dean.

But, sometimes, a near-fifty, much-battered and abused, skinny and arthritic body just has to stop pretending to be eighteen again. When it takes longer to get dressed—in ankle stabilizers, knee braces, wrist straps, safety bifocals, and multiple sweatbands—than it does to play, a body has to stop and think. When the weekly cost of muscle relaxers and painkillers exceeds the exorbitant price of high-topped basketball shoes, when midnight muscle cramps are the after effects of every scrimmage, maybe it's time to retire.

I did not think it all through and arrive at a rational decision to turn in my locker. A three-month battle with bronchitis sidelined me, and after three or four weeks I realized that my ankle wasn't swollen and throbbing anymore, that my oft-broken little finger didn't ache, that I could actually walk without limping and sleep without charley horses.

My pharmaceutical bill dropped to nearly nothing.

My grandsons turned three years old.

So I made the big step. I cleaned out the locker, had it fumigated, gave the Converse shoes to a younger brother, and threw away the assortment of orthopedic appliances, the five-dollar-a-pair socks, and the mildewed purple gym bag.

I kept the Lakers warm-up jacket.

I tossed the liniment, the Ben Gay, and the finger splints, quit having all my friends collect Motrin coupons.

Now I eat lunch with my wife.

She doesn't smell like sweat and old socks, and she isn't as likely to hit me across the nose with an elbow.

But she *is* a former cheerleader, so I haven't given up the game altogether.

Rooster-from-Hell Sent Home

I've never liked hens or chickens, except fried, baked, or broiled, but for some reason my mother's flock of bantams ("banty" to us) particularly irked me. The colorful miniatures were good-for-nothing, too scrawny to eat, and their aggressive tempers as they pecked, strutted, and clucked around the barnyard rubbed me the wrong way.

The strident little rooster was a natural warrior, but back then I didn't know about cockfighting so I didn't put him to any good use. But even the arrogant, angry, loud little rooster couldn't protect the hens from all the weasels, foxes, possums, and stray dogs, so gradually his flock thinned.

Finally, the rooster was the only one left.

Maybe he was lonesome, or maybe he was just trying to pick a fight, but that shrill little demon would flap up onto the fence post outside our bedroom window every morning at 4 A.M. and greet the morning two hours too early.

And even a miniature rooster can rattle the windowpanes.

We yelled at him, threw shoes, and threatened worse.

But the strutting intruder belonged to my mother, whose potential for warfare was even greater than the rooster's, so the varmint lived on.

For a while longer.

Growing boys can't go without sleep forever.

So one morning, just as the rooster-from-hell flapped his wings and reared back to cut loose, we shot him.

With the little .22, using shots that made only a soft "pop," we cut that rooster down in mid-screech.

We crawled out the bedroom window, carried the corpse a half mile down the holler, buried him under some rocks, then crept back into the bedroom for some rare uninterrupted sleep.

We never did confess. I still haven't. Four brothers slept in that bedroom, and I refuse to identify the trigger man.

My wife's chicken story isn't so final. Her miniatures were pets, such as any boneheaded chicken can be a pet, so when the family moved from the country into town she insisted that her banties go too.

In a scene right out of *Grapes of Wrath* (or maybe *The Beverly Hillbillies*) the roosters were caught and caged, then the wooden cages were strapped to the top of the old car.

But there was a railroad crossing at the edge of town. The car lurched, the ropes broke, the cages fell, the little flock of squawking country roosters scattered.

The adventures of the country roosters in town would have made a good Disney movie, but there was a sobbing, stubborn little girl who wanted her pet chickens back.

So her father chased them down, one by one, surely swearing under his breath the whole time and hoping none of his friends would come along and witness him chasing chickens along the railroad track.

This is the same little girl who had a pet pig and a goat who pulled her along in a cart, who was afraid of cows but wanted to get friendly with an old yellow-toothed, ill-tempered mule.

We haven't kept chickens or goats during our twenty years together, just neurotic Siamese cats, an eighty-pound Dalmatian who wanted to be carried, a beagle who stole shoes, and a stray mongrel named "Cousin" (he came to visit one Sunday and never left).

I've never been sure whether our animals were strange when we got them or if me made them that way; the monster cat Hydra lived fifteen or sixteen years, destroyed six cornshuck chairs, two sofas, and one entire basement, and we still grieved when she died.

And while I might feel a twinge of guilt over helping murder my mother's little rooster, I sure don't feel any grief.

Waitresses Are Real People

Some of my favorite people in the whole wide world are restaurant waitresses, even the ones who call me "hon" and assume I drink sweetened ice tea.

I know the term "waitress" is an outdated, sexist term. In the plastic, gimmicky, chain restaurant world they have "servers," a term I personally find much more degrading, and most "servers" provide detached, methodical service void of any warmth or personality. Or they try too hard to entertain, for tips, and that's even worse than the robotic approach.

The stereotypical southern waitress, the gum-popping, syrupy-voiced, sassy-but-sweet soul of good humor and tireless effort, *does* still exist in the truck stops and roadside cafes of the Sunbelt, the places where I prefer to eat because some of them still serve food you can taste, but the good waitress is totally out of place in modern fast-food operations.

I can't help the way I am. I *like* being greeted with a smile or friendly insult and a chipped white mug full of strong coffee, by a confident and outgoing earthy personality whose no-nonsense approach gets my food to me fast. A good southern waitress would not be at all intimidated if President Bush came by for the roast beef special, and he'd get no better service than anybody else. And he'd not get as good treatment as that which is given to regular customers.

If he got lucky, and business was slow, the president might get an insight into local politics and weather, might get tipped off as to which pies are fresh and which are frozen, might get to learn what it's like to work for a living doing something you love to do.

Contrary to what a handful of blustery, insecure, pushy little people think, waitresses are human. And some of them won't put up with any hint of treatment that is contrary to normal; one of my all-time favorite waitresses once offered an obnoxious patron a whole pot of hot coffee—pot and all on top of his head—if he said one more degrading word. He, wisely, believed her and became the soul of courtesy.

In a little South Carolina diner, we once breakfasted on country ham, eggs, and potatoes, prepared and served by a tiny waitress who didn't even write the order down but knew exactly what we owed when it was time to pay, who explained good naturedly that the cook hadn't come to work and she was having to run the whole place that morning "all by my oneself."

And, all by her oneself, she gave much better food and service than the expensive hotel restaurant of the evening before.

Pretty young girls watch the professionals and learn how to work customers for tips, but a real southern waitress enjoys her work. She's on a first-name basis with every regular customer, remembers travelers from previous trips, tolerates the outrageous flirting, but could cut off a hand placed on the wrong part of her anatomy. Ask her what's good and believe her; she *knows* what goes on back in the kitchen.

Whenever I travel to New York City I gravitate to the hole-in-the-wall diners, especially for breakfast, for all the bustle, noise, smells, and the unbelievably fast and expert work done by the cook at the sizzling grill.

He (all of them I've seen are men) will juggle eggs, ham, potatoes, pancakes, bacon strips, buttered toast, and a dozen orders all at once, and run a loud, never-ending monologue with the cops, dancers, tourists, hookers, and stockbrokers who fight for a spot at the counter.

After breakfast at John's Diner near Lincoln Center I have enough belief that New Yorkers are human to get me through a day in the inhuman parts of the city.

I like people who like their work and are good at what they do, be they waitresses, short-order cooks, bankers, or politicians.

But there's a special place in my heart for all the world's waitresses.

Right up there with my wife, my mother, and my kids.

Real people, every one of them.

Learning Horse Sense the Hard Way

From the time I can remember, I worked a team of horses. We pulled the turning plow, sulky cultivator, tobacco setter, wagon, hay rake, mower, and everything else on the late O. V. Doyle's Bluebank farm with his teams; Mr. Doyle hated for any machine with motor-driven wheels to touch his acreage, where we grew tobacco on the shares, and to do the work he kept an assortment of big draft horses.

Mr. Doyle's favorite mare, Maude, was the best of the bunch, a big, good-natured bay equally at home dragging a wagonload of hay, plodding slowly with the tobacco setter, or doubling as a saddle horse. Patrick was a huge black gelding who hated to go slow, who'd fight the reins and drag along whatever other horse was hitched with him.

My team, for years, was a pair of little matched grays, a mare and a gelding. But then the gelding died, and the only horse Mr. Doyle could find the right size was another mare, so I wound up working Kate and Beck. Normally they were a docile, well-mannered pair, but then one summer they both came in heat at the same time.

For three weeks I was harassed, kicked, and bit at every turn. I tried to tie their heads off in opposite directions. I had to walk down the tongue of the John Deere mower to hook up the trace chains, and back then I was young and agile enough to dodge most of the oversized hooves that flew at me. I wasn't old enough then to exactly understand just what "in heat" meant, but to this day I associate the term with bruises, big yellow teeth, grunts and squeals, and ill-tempered female horses.

My job at daybreak every day was to harness two teams—four big horses—and I wasn't tall enough to reach up to their broad backs. I stood on a box to sling the harness over, then crawled around and under a half ton of horse to fasten all the hooks, snaps, and buckles. I got stepped on at least twice each morning, but horse manure and straw are pretty good cushioning.

Some stuff I had to learn the hard way. Nobody told me, at first, that "whoa" to a team standing still meant to back up. So one afternoon I screamed "whoa" at the top of my lungs, frantic and bleeding, until the team had me backed snugly halfway through a three-strand barbed wire fence. The more I yelled, the more they backed up, the deeper the bloodied barbs cut. My father ran from the other side of the field to save my life and explain just how it is that you put a team of horses in reverse.

One cold early March Saturday morning, my father left me two miles from the house with three shaggy, out-of-shape horses hitched to a riding plow, with a five-acre field to turn under. The horses were fat and lazy from a winter of inactivity, the plow flipped over every time the point caught a rock, the ground was half frozen, and then it started spitting snow. In six hours I plowed almost six furrows around the field. When Daddy finally came back for me I was frozen, sniffling, numb, muddy head-to-toe, and totally convinced that we needed a tractor.

He stuck me in the car to thaw out and went to show me how you were supposed to plow. He lasted about half a furrow. A neighbor came over Monday with a Farmall and turned the field for us.

One Spring Mr. Doyle brought home a sassy young saddle mare, a high-strung filly with a nasty habit of biting anybody who looked the other way. She got me that fall, as I swung down out of the barn after hanging two loads of tobacco up against a blistering tin roof. I hit the ground swatting leaves, sweat, and tobacco worms, sucked in some cooler air, then jumped about ten feet when I got bit from behind, a hearty chomp on bare shoulders and back. I turned around, doubled up a fist, and popped that mare a good one, right in her tender nose.

The next thing I remember seeing was shiny little sharp horseshoes and flailing feet, way up above my head. The mare meant to hit back. Daddy swears I cleared a woven wire fence with three strands of wire on top by a foot, Michael Jordan in jeans and brogans, with a set of horse teeth about a foot from my behind.

We worked those horses from the time I was eight or nine years old until the summer before my senior year in college. To me, the horses were great big pets, my buddies, oversized babies whose feelings got hurt if I raised my voice; thousand-pound puppies who'd roll and play at the end of the day's work and make the earth shake.

When Mr. Doyle finally sold the farm, the deal included his horses. They were to be fed, cared for, and not worked, allowed to live out their days there. I don't know how long old Maude lived, but she'd earned her retirement, and I'm sure she told the other horses exactly what to do as they lounged around and watched everybody else work.

I Survived My Father's Home Remedies

In recent years much has been written about the healing wonders of folk medicine, the poultices and potions concocted from barks, berries, leaves, and mystery, the unexplainable therapeutic values of the old mountain voodoo-like medical treatments.

Lots of them worked. My grandfather was sort of a medicine man, a treater of copperhead bites, burns, cuts, bullet wounds, warts, colds, or whatever else might ail a family member or neighbor. Somewhere, we hope, Granddaddy's old notebook of remedies still exists.

But, a generation removed from my grandfather, I was more likely to get dosed with castor oil, doused in turpentine or coal oil, or treated with tobacco juice, liniment, whiskey, or some sort of patent salve. Fortunately, my brothers and sisters and I were basically healthy enough to outlive the treatments.

When I got stung by a lumbering bumblebee, my step-grandfather quickly applied a juicy wad of chewing tobacco. Unfortunately, I'd been stung just above the eye. My juice-scalded eyeball *did* hurt so bad that I forgot all about being stung, so in a way the treatment worked. And, in a week or so, I regained most of my vision.

We all quickly learned to conceal any stomach or bowel upsets. Vile, thick, foul, slimy, stinking castor oil, two or three tablespoons full, was standard treatment for whatever ailed you. Early preventive medicine is the best description for castor oil; anybody who'd ever swallowed a full dose simply *refused* to ever get sick again. Or, if you did, you hid in the outhouse or barn and hoped you'd get well before anybody noticed.

For most cuts and scrapes, out came the turpentine or coal oil (that's kerosene to you city folks), and I can attest to the healing power of both fluids. Wounds treated with either turpentine or coal oil heal quickly, cleanly, without scars.

When I once wrecked my bicycle and slid thirty feet across rough asphalt on my elbows, my father took it one step farther. He coated my skinless parts with roofing tar, sticky black pitch, a more than generous application. I spent the next week trying to get it off. Either the pitch or the coal oil I used to soak it off healed the injuries. With no scarring.

Poison ivy was and is the bane of an active country kid's existence, and there's still nothing better than a baking soda paste to cure the itch.

Wondrous baking soda. It defuses insect stings, heals poison ivy rash, cleans the teeth, absorbs odors, settles the stomach, and even is used for some sort of cooking.

About ten years ago, though, after a heavy Sunday dinner and too little activity, I couldn't sleep. Indigestion, gas, a bloated stomach, and nowhere in the house was there a handy jar of antacid tablets. "Go take two big spoons of baking soda and a glass of water," advised my wife.

After thirty more minutes of misery, I agreed it was worth a try. I stumbled downstairs, gagged down two tablespoons full, chased it with two glasses of water, and came back to bed.

After a few minutes, it was obvious the magic wasn't working. I was worse. I was swollen, bloated, gasping for breath. I'm not one to suffer in total silence. "You're the worst doctor I've ever been to," I grumbled to my wife. "I think you've killed me."

She, puzzled, offered sympathy but could not understand what had gone wrong.

"It's that damned baking powder," I wailed.

She got a strange look on her face. "Baking *powder*?" she asked.

"Yes," I gasped. "Baking powder. Two spoons full and two glasses of water, just like you said."

She started giggling.

I started cussing, best as I could under the circumstances.

"I said baking *soda*," she gasped through tears of laughter. "*Soda.* Not powder."

"What the hell's the difference?" I snorted.

She dissolved, hugged her belly, and laughed until she fell out of her chair.

Obviously, I survived the long night.

But I learned better than to try and make biscuits without a mixing bowl and oven, and learned the difference between baking soda and baking powder.

Now, whenever I feel a little bloated, I just drink me a Pepsi.

But somehow I doubt if they'll ever ask me to do a commercial.

Nights Dreams Are Made Of

Reading about today's high school proms, about the ballrooms, tuxedos, limos, three-hundred-dollar gowns, hotel rooms, and catered breakfasts, reminded me of a night I'd almost forgotten.

Of an evening over thirty years ago, of my first ever formal date. I was sixteen, a junior at Fleming County High School, proud owner of a brand-new license to drive and precious little else. I don't remember how the date got arranged, but I assume there had to be a middleman. I could never have openly asked. But my date was pretty, probably fifteen, and likely no more prepared for a formal evening than I was.

To be safe we double-dated. My friend from town, I figured, was much more suave and able to keep up a conversation. What I didn't know was that his date lived halfway across the county, up a farm road even more washed-out and winding than the ones I was used to.

I don't remember what I wore, but my date's new gown was low-cut enough to where I just handed her mother the corsage. My fumbling hands would have ended the evening then and there. Our tiny gym was decorated with crepe paper, tables, and awkward couples in uneasy dress clothes. We never danced. I couldn't, she couldn't, we wouldn't. We stayed to the bitter end.

Then the night got more exciting. Getting my friend's date home on time, halfway to nowhere, was a mad rush, and then coming down the hillside I dragged the muffler off my father's old 1951 Dodge. In dress clothes, in pitch-black darkness, I broke off rusted wire from a fence and tied the pipes up off the ground. Exhaust bellowing, at 3 A.M. in the morning, I frantically gunned the Dodge up the driveway to my anxious date's house.

The porch light was on. The living room light was on. The kitchen light was on. I couldn't see him, but I just knew her frothing father was lurking with a loaded double-barreled shotgun. I reached over and opened the passenger-side door. My date fled. I was halfway home before she got to the porch steps.

There was no obvious pursuit.

My date and I shared classrooms and hallways for more than another year and never, ever, discussed our one night out.

A year later I was a relatively sophisticated high school senior, president of the school's student council, college-bound, owner of a slightly yellowed, secondhand white dinner jacket, and my prom date was the most beautiful girl in Fleming County. My girlfriend's father provided his new Buick for the evening. The prom was a swirl of sound, friendship, and color, then we drove over into Ohio for hamburgers. We cruised back up into Kentucky with the windows open, the moon shining in, and Roy Orbison's "Only the Lonely" wailing on the radio. I probably was, for the first time in my life, absolutely certain all was well and wonderful with the world.

Before I'd left home earlier that evening, I'd told my mother that if I was elected king of the prom I'd leave my crown on her sewing machine so she'd know.

My mother still has that cardboard and tinfoil headpiece.

But the king of the prom, the smug high school senior whose world was a sudden dazzle of wonder, spent the whole next day plowing out the corn patch, riding a horse-drawn sulky cultivator down endless long rows.

But somehow I didn't smell the sweaty mares, wasn't aware of the dust on my faded clothes, my swollen, sleepless eyes, or my riveted old work shoes.

Because I still was, in my mind, adrift in the glitter and wonder of the senior prom, of the grandest night I'd ever known, of soft spring moonlight and Roy Orbison's music, of that first simple and stirring step into a very different world.

So if you've ever wondered why they have senior proms, I think I just told you.

Wedding Bell(bottom) Blues: My Baby Girl Is Getting Married

Well, she's still a baby to me, even if she is twenty-two years old, a veteran of four years on her own, and about to graduate from college and become a physician assistant.

And, because she's my baby, she's getting away with ruining my reputation for being a blue-jeaned old hermit, a sort of old redneck hippie who disdains and avoids all ceremony and anything else that requires dressing up.

There will be a church wedding. A rehearsal dinner. Bridesmaids and a ring bearer (my grandson Brian, already an old hand at such as that). Newspaper announcements. Pictures.

A tuxedo for the father of the bride.

You rent the things, Beth says. Fitted, formal, complete with the frilly shirt, bow tie, striped britches, and sash around the belly.

And plastic shoes.

They must be plastic, I figure, to be that shiny.

My wife has already told me I'll have to buy a pair of dress socks, too. No gym socks, she says, nor the heavy Levis I've worn for twenty years.

No purple shoelaces.

No cap, not even my silky, dress-up "Peterbilt" model that's got the chromed snaps.

What, I ask, about underwear? Clean, wife and daughter agree.

There'll also be a fresh haircut for me, I'm told, and my fingernails will be checked. No smudged glasses. No patchy shave, no hair in my nose and ears.

Maybe a girdle, too, somebody suggests, eyeing my gut.

I ignore that.

Everybody sure does seem to be enjoying the prospect of watching me squirm in formal clothes. Enjoying it too much.

Once, I remind them, I owned a three-piece suit.

True, says my wife, but it was faded denim with bellbottom pants, wide lapels, and shiny buttons. You wore high-heeled boots with it, she added, and had hair down to your shoulders. But the outfit *did* bring five dollars in a yard sale, she remembers.

And she thinks she saw somebody wearing it last Halloween.

I can handle the whole thing, I tell everybody, as long as the place is air-conditioned.

Nobody responds to that.

The wedding is in late August. Dog days. Temperatures of 105 degrees. Humidity.

Sweat. Lots of it.

I'm a world-class competitor in perspiration. We all know that. Nobody in his right mind would rent dress clothes to me in August.

The church is air-conditioned, decides my daughter.

Which means if it isn't already it will be by August. My daughter is as stubborn as I am. I just hope I don't get a bill, in September, from a Fleming County heating and air-conditioning contractor.

We haven't even talked wedding presents yet. For sure, Beth will get legal title to her little red car. Plus the insurance bills. But

I suspect she'll want more. Like toasters and microwaves, fancy little goblets, and spoons that match. Maybe a good mop and a toilet brush. A three-legged iron kettle for heating the wash water. A good double-bitted axe.

I don't think she has any aprons, either.

But I'll worry about those gifts later. Before then, there's her birthday and college graduation. By the end of summer, I may have to sell her little red car to get money for the tuxedo rental.

Or, more likely, sell my own car and take out a third mortgage on the house.

I'll wear the tux, though, when I go see the bankers.

It ought to impress them, too.

Washing Clothes in the Creek

My mother, who climbed up on a chair to mix and bake her first chocolate cake when she was five years old, who did the family wash in the waters of Caney Creek from about the same age, recalls those early years at Gimlet in Elliott County with happy laughter and a sentimental tear or two.

The washing was a daylight-to-dark affair. It started before dawn, with a load of laundry on the low sled pulled by the two small black steers her brothers had trained to the yoke, and spanned the day, until late afternoon when the plodding miniature oxen would return to haul the clean sheets, shirts, and worn out little girl back to the homeplace.

When Granddaddy would go out for a night, horseback across the ridge to sing and maybe drink a little moonshine, my mother would lie awake and wait for the rhythmic clop-clop-clop of the saddle mare's swinging pace and the raspy, happy songs of her father to let her know he'd made it home alive once more.

My mother and one of her brothers cooked the family breakfast every morning for so many years that—the morning after my mother's wedding—Grandma responded to Granddaddy's request that she get up and cook him some breakfast with a puzzled, "Why, Mark, I don't rightly know as I remember how."

My mother weighed eighty-two pounds when her second

child was born. I was the third, delivered by a young aunt just before my father left for World War II; until his return she took care of us all by herself, survived the gun battle just outside our front door and whatever else the remote mountain world threw at a pretty young woman alone with three babies.

We moved away from Elliott County to a farm in Fleming County, and I grew up awed by my mother's ability to get things done.

To move the heat stove out of the living room after winter was over, the tiny woman literally greased the skids: she cut four slices of pork rind—the tough outer skin, greasy on the inner side—and put one slice under each stove leg. The big cast-iron Warm Morning heat stove, 150 pounds heavier than my mother, slid easily through the house to its summer storage in the pantry.

She cut our hair with hand-squeezed clippers; sewed my sisters' dresses (without store-bought patterns) on her old foot-powered Singer; canned probably five hundred quarts of beans, corns, tomatoes, and blackberries every summer; cooked three meals a day; heated wash water in a backyard kettle; and kept nine healthy, rowdy, and rambunctious kids under control.

Somewhere she managed to find money for those few special things; a dollar or two to slip into the letters she sent me when I went away to college to finish paying for the sports coat I laid away then couldn't afford to bail out.

My mother has never looked or acted her age. I took a gymnastics class, went home at Christmas to show off my physical skills, and got out-performed by a lithe and limber middle-aged woman in a cotton housedress who'd never heard of a PE class.

She called me a few years later to see if I had any plans to come home from North Carolina anytime soon, then told me my dog was dying, and she kept him alive long enough for me to make the trip and say goodbye.

In her fifties my mother learned to drive, found a job, and started a new life; she inspired my short story "The Liberation of Elsie Watts," and the fictional series that is now twenty stories long.

She was named Fleming County's "Woman of the Year," and in my favorite picture she is wearing her award sash.

Just like Miss America.

But the last time she came to visit—bringing a grandchild to enroll at Berea College—my mother confessed that she'd never been able to do the wash just right, way back then in Caney Creek.

She never did, she said, learn how to properly wring out a sheet in the cold creek water.

The vision of a determined little girl, waterlogged sheets, a team of little black steers yoked to a sled, and clear waters splashing against smooth rocks, somehow seemed impossible. More like something from another century or a dreamy scene from a John Fox Jr. novel.

But I promised my mother I'd never tell that she didn't learn to wring out the sheets.

So don't repeat a word of this.

Little Sam's Last Good Deed: I Do Get Attached to My Pets

Unreasonably so, sometimes.

My favorite dog, after childhood, was a peculiar beagle named "Sam," actually "Sam II," who shared three good years with us.

Sam was a slightly oversized beagle, a half brother to the original Sam, who came to me from the same hillside barn near Disputana, Kentucky. Somebody stole Sam-the-first, a too-trusting hound, during rabbit season. But son-of-Sam would not have gone off happily with a stranger.

He was—and he knew it—the number one pet of the household, the personal favorite of the big guy who dished out the food. Sam's partner, the huge Dalmatian Portia, conceded that Sam was the top dog despite her hundred-pound weight advantage.

Theirs was a two-way relationship, though. When the eleven Dalmatian puppies arrived, chewed all the hair and hide off their mother's belly, and drove her a few steps closer to insanity, it was little Sam who took over.

He became the chief baby-sitter and playmate for a litter of aggressive pups who were, by the time they were a month old, as big as he was. Sam provided the rough-and-tumble play for the pups, napped under a layer of black-and-white furballs, took care of the babies so the mother could recover her strength.

Sam and Portia were the inseparable odd couple—the short-legged, flop-eared beagle and the broad-chested Dalmatian—but Sam knew he had special rights with me. He loved weekends, would scratch at the kitchen door to come inside, and crawl, as he'd done since he was a tiny pup, under my chair to share the morning coffee and newspaper.

For years after he was gone, I'd automatically reach down under my seat to scratch Sam's ears, to hear his contented sighs and groans.

Sam also loved the old off-road Honda motorcycle and would run himself to exhaustion every time it fired up. Short legs pumping, long ears flying, frenzied high-pitched yips loud above the roar of the engine, Sam would run at my foot, nipping at the footpegs, until I'd finally give it up and park to prevent a canine heart attack.

Little Sam also stunk. There's just no polite way to say it. Somebody once told me dogs based their social status upon smell, and if that's true Sam was surely a king. His normal, everyday aroma was simply awful, and sometimes he'd reach out for even greater accomplishments.

My daughter once explained Sam's distinctive aura: "Sam found a dead cow up on the hill," she announced happily, "and he crawled all the way up in it to eat."

Not even I, that Saturday, could stomach any intimacy with little Sam.

Sam was about three when some idiot in a battered green van deliberately swerved off the highway to hit him. One of the kids saw, called, and I came home to bury my warm, unmarked buddy in a grave in the corner of the yard.

When the Dalmatian tried to dig up her old friend, I had to put a temporary cover of cement blocks over Sam.

I also, after some hours of brooding and bourbon, loaded my rifle and sat by the roadside waiting for a battered green van. Which, thankfully, didn't come by.

About a year later my daughter was learning to solo on her big brother's new small Honda bike when she lost control and crashed. By the time I got there, Beth was crawling out of the bushes, scratched and muddy, bawling helplessly.

I thought she'd hurt herself.

No, Beth assured me, sobbing and sniffling, she wasn't damaged.

But, she pointed out, wailing anew, when she'd wrecked the Honda she'd landed on Sam's grave.

"Did I hurt Sam?" she wondered, wiping tears.

I assured her that nothing would have pleased little Sam more than to have been there to cushion her fall.

She liked that answer.

So did I.

Political Correctness Un-American

Political correctness is getting out of control.

Or, maybe, it's getting too much *in* control.

In control of too much of our language, too much of our culture, too much of the effort we all have to make in our daily lives.

It borders on the absurd.

Of course, being either an Appalachian-American or Kentucky-American, two distinct ethnic/economic/accented minorities as yet officially unrecognized, I read with interest the words Daniel J. Boorstin wrote for *Parade* magazine July 25, 1993.

"I think," wrote Boorstin, "that the notion of a hyphenated-American—whether Polish-American, Italian-American or African-American—is un-American."

He's correct, of course,

But not politically correct.

And political correctness often removes much of the beauty from the English language.

For over 135 years, the official Berea College seal read: "God hath made of one blood all nations of men."

A leading-edge liberal arts college must, of course, always be politically correct, so the newly adopted wording on the seal is "God has made of one blood all peoples of the earth."

Couldn't they, I wonder, at least have hung on to "hath"?

As a reader-American who once was a student-American (and sometimes functions as a writer-American), I love the language of the King James version of the Old Testament; the flowing elegance and direct insight of William Shakespeare; Thomas

Jefferson's preamble to the U.S. Constitution; the opening lines of Lincoln's Gettysburg Address.

Most of the time, the very same scholars who so advocate political correctness in the use of the language are also the worst offenders when it comes to the use of popular academic jargon and a stuffy insider vocabulary, casually tossing out words like "pedagogy" (which means, I suspect, "I have a Ph.D. Do you?") and "ambience" (which means pretty much whatever you'd like for it to mean).

Recently I spent two full days meeting with a room full of folklorists, and could have used an interpreter. No "folk" in this world would have understood any part of the lengthy discourses, not even the numerous references to Native-Americans and African-Americans.

Redneck-American that I am sometimes, I was sorely tempted to offer up some barnyard-American language. Some muledriver-American jargon.

But I didn't.

And I chuckled whenever, in the heat of discussion, the group would forget and use the once correct terms "Indian" and "black" until someone would notice and make the necessary political correction.

I also discovered, during these meetings, that the Appalachian craft revival is now being studied and promoted as a "women's movement."

That's true, in many ways, but I doubt that many of the women actually involved saw it that way. They didn't discriminate against the men who were working with them. They *all* referred to themselves, back then, as "craftsmen," and the surviving craftspeople still do.

Supportive as I am of the gender equalization effort, and of due recognition to all ethnic groups, I cling to elements of some politically incorrect but beautifully stated language.

Like "God hath made of one blood all nations of men."

Sometimes, tradition and grace outweigh political correctness, and the simple elegance of the English language is more important than how today's culture chooses to interpret words out of their historical context.

A Salute to Women Who Cut Up

One of the most newsworthy knifing stories of the year involves the woman who filleted her estranged husband's privates.

That's not exactly the wording they used in the news service articles, but they did spell out that she used a twelve-inch filet knife. That, after being raped, she waited until he went to sleep and then removed a significant portion of his offending anatomy. Then realized, some distance down the road, that she still had the filet of privates with her, rolled down the car window, and tossed it.

She did get worried, later, and called the police. Told them where to locate the missing portion. The police searched the dark intersection, found the filet, packed it in ice for the trip to the hospital. A surgeon worked nine hours to reattach the severed appendage.

Police promptly arrested the knife-wielding woman, who surely now wishes there'd been a hungry stray dog snuffing around at the intersection where she unloaded the fresh meat. If convicted, she could serve up to forty years.

I think she deserves, instead, a medal.

Crossed filet knives cast in bronze, maybe.

Her husband, who cannot be charged for rape under that state's laws, will likely go scot-free.

Almost.

There *is* the small matter of his physical and mental trauma. Probably lots of future mental and physical therapy.

Hopefully, he will not emulate the late President Lyndon B. Johnson and go on TV to show off his scar. Except, given the lack of taste displayed daily by Geraldo and Sally Jessie, I fully expect to see the deserving victim paid handsomely to spill out his story in gory detail to a national audience. To tell all in the supermarket tabloids, to play himself in the low-budget, made-for-TV movie.

Nobody I know would be willing to serve as his double for the filming.

The reactions to this infamous incident are interesting. Lots of men cringe, turn pale, and change the subject. They probably go home to hide the kitchen cutlery and sleep in separate, locked bedrooms. Stop eating steak, cleaning fish, or slicing bologna.

I haven't observed any women expressing sympathy for the poor rapist. Lots of gleeful chuckles, smirks, and ribald remarks, even some speculation as to what matter of physical therapy will be employed. As to whether a serrated steak knife, old fashioned butcher knife, or a pair of poultry shears would have made a cleaner cut.

Should the knifewoman go to trial, the jury selection process is (pardon the too-obvious pun) cut and dried. The prosecution will want macho men with beer bellies, boots, and Budweiser belt buckles. The defense will look for wild-eyed feminist activists.

However this bizarre cut-and-run incident ends, both the men and the women of this country have been given a message. To the men, it's obvious: don't force your attentions where they're unwanted. You could be the next victim of the unkindest cut of all.

Women get reinforcement in the need to speak up, fight back, to put an end to sexual abuse.

The method of fighting back used in this instance may be, admittedly, just a little extreme. A cut above normal. A blow below the belt.

But if they'll put me on the jury, I'll vote for acquittal.

I've always been partial to a cutup.

Defining the "Head of the Holler"

Somebody asked me the other day just what "Head of the Holler" means.

It's sort of complicated.

In these parts a "holler" is what I reckon they'd call a "hollow" in other places, sort the of the way a possum is an "opossum" in parts of the world.

But you *could* call a holler a valley, or maybe a cove, but whatever you call it, a holler is the low place between two hills or mountains and most of the time there's a creek (or, at home, a "crick") splashing down through the middle.

Follow the "crick" far enough upstream, climb high enough, go far enough back into the hills, and you'll finally come to the "head of the holler."

It's as far back as you can go.

Where it all begins.

But, for my purposes, "head of the holler" is more of a state of mind than a geographical designation.

It's the end result of growing up rural, remote, removed, maybe even a little reluctant to let the outside world in or to venture down and see what's out there.

It's a point of view, shaped by a lifetime.

It's roots, twined deep into rocky hillsides, and a self-determining will to survive.

A wry awareness that, no matter how bad it gets, it could get worse.

And probably will.

That the basic answer to it all is a sort of cussed endurance, a little more work and a little less luxury, a will to survive no matter what the world dishes out, the leathery toughness to roll with the punches and stagger back up, bloodied but still fighting.

And still laughing.

I laugh best when I laugh at me, at my own "quareness" and peculiarities, at the pratfalls of a redneck blundering off through a world designed and directed by people who've never slept on a feather bed, never fetched water from a spring, never lived life at the head of the holler back before the hollers were all full of new A-frames cut into hillsides better suited to red foxes and copperheads.

And I haven't lived that way in a long, long, time.

I don't intend to, either, ever again.

I *like* running water, gas furnaces, hospitals, telephones, air conditioners, and cable television, enjoy not having to split wood, butcher hogs, work a team of horses, or sleep in an unheated bedroom.

The physical changes are welcome.

Some of the other changes aren't.

I still prefer the simple language, the directness, the practical reliability of people from the head of the holler, the people who say what they mean and mean what they say.

Who don't pretend, don't try to impress, don't want any handouts, favors, or special treatment.

Who feel free to laugh out loud, right out in public.

But I also don't deny reality, don't refuse to acknowledge that much of what I remember and write about is no longer around.

Not even at the head of the most remote holler.

The very same forces that brought us the highways, hospitals, housing, and TV sets also brought the end of a special way of living.

That just leaves a generation of us to remember.

To wonder what happened.

To, in my case, wrestle with writing about making the adjustment, about moving from the head of the holler into an urban neighborhood, from simplicity to complexity, from a rocking chair on the back porch to a computerized workstation.

But, in my head and heart, in my basic instincts, in my outlook on life, I still live at the "head of the holler."

By choice.

Pigs 4 Sale

There's a bent willow sign nailed to the deck across the front of our house that says "Pigs 4 Sale."

We don't really sell pigs. The sign has absolutely no significance.

We just like it.

The sign was a gift from a good friend, a joke at the weary end of the New York gift show.

Another N.Y. exhibitor gave me the "Thou shalt not whine" sign for my office. That one does have significance.

But "Pigs 4 Sale" is purely fun. A sort of redneck remnant. Like my affinity for sweaty old caps, rusty pickup trucks, hound dogs, and people who don't pretend to be anything except exactly what they are.

And I'll confess, right off, that I'm not one of those rare, delightful people lucky enough to always feel free to cuss when they're mad and scratch when they itch.

With apologies to Little Jimmy Dickens, whose song I paraphrased, I envy those who can be what they are.

Most of us can't afford that directness.

We have to act out whatever role we've chosen or been assigned.

That's not all bad.

It pays the bills, for one thing. Opens doors, offers glimpses into other worlds. Explains different ways.

Different, not better.

Anybody who grows up Appalachian, black, or just plain old poor is handed, early on, some pretty blunt realities.

Life ain't easy.

And it ain't fair.

But on a wall in my home is an etching of a clump of grapes. There are words, too. "Sour grapes make good wine."

A friend brought me the print at one of life's low points.

And, then, I needed the daily reminder.

Most of the time, I don't need it.

My daughter's elegant wedding was, in many ways, a poignant reminder of just how much life has changed. Marching down the aisle in a tux, guiding a beautiful young woman who's also a medical professional, I couldn't help but to think back.

To early years in Elliott County, Kentucky, to a time and place light years removed from mainstream America.

To the crowded little farmhouse at Bald Hill, the sometimes hopelessness of poverty, the mixed comfort and resentment of the familiar words: "God must love poor people, He made so many of us."

To almost fifty years of intense effort, tough times, triumphs, and bleak despair.

To fifty years of rejection, of a smug world trying to tell me I have to conform.

That my ways, my people, and my heritage are somehow deficient.

That my language, my music, my religious practices, and my very core are less than acceptable.

That I ought to know my place and stay in it.

Marching slowly down that aisle, looking down at my son, grandson, and soon-to-be son-in-law, I wondered how I ever wound up where I am, wondered if some memories of earlier years are actually real, wondered if life would be easier for these new generations.

Wondered if any of them could ever really understand.

If they could know why it's so important to me to cling to some old habits, to hang a "Pigs 4 Sale" sign across my house, to retreat to country music and time alone when the world gets too crowded.

I guess I *do* know my place, after all.

I just wish I could stay there all the time.

Part 4

Looking

Many Hands Make Light Work

Looking back, and trying to look forward, I have very mixed emotions about our abused homeland, with particular concern for troubled eastern Kentucky.

Everywhere, I see problems: incoming garbage, rampant unemployment, poor scholastic achievement, corrupt politics, human misery, and hopelessness. A character in my sarcastic short story, "The Bitter Creek Appalachian Symposium," reads his narrative poem, "Bitter Creek Breakdown," to a suitably rowdy audience, and in those verses expresses much of my mixed feeling about our region and its situation:

Up here on Bitter Creek
The water runs green and acid yellow
Clogged by Pampers and Clorox jugs
Refrigerators and shells of old Chevrolets.

The government run us a water line
In 1968, so we got a mobile home,
And Uncle John's Black Lung check
Pays the bills
Ever since we voted wet
And a body can't make a living no more
Bootlegging.

Cousin Jeff grows marijuana
Over on Poosey Mountain
But he says it's hard to make any cash money.
Last year some old boys from Hazard stole half his crop
And this year the cows got in
And et it.

They give mighty good milk for a while,
Jeff said,
But then they got all sniffly and red-eyed
Went to wearing red bandannas
And writing poetry.
Brother Ben went to Vietnam
And come home a hippie.
Beard, hair
Old Army field jackets
And a strange look in his eyes.

But now they made him a memorial
Over in Frankfort
And the lottery, it's going to get Ben a hundred-dollar bonus
So I guess it's okay
That he still don't sleep at night
Can't hear out of one ear
Or hold down a job.

There's work up around Lexington, they say
If a body'll drive two hours each way
Build Japanese cars
Or sweep up floors for one of the coal companies
That owns most of this county.

No work here, though.
Mines are about shut down,
Timber's all cut,
And the government's idea of how to get us all back to work
Is to have us make quilts, whittle, spin and weave,
And peddle our stuff to the tourists.

Ain't no tourists here, though.

And factories, they say,
Won't come to the mountains.
Bad roads, bad water, bad schools,
And we're all too damned ornery to work
When it's squirrel season.

So here on Bitter Creek
We got to go it on our own
Scrounge out a living somehow
Hang onto this hillside
And eighty acres of scrub timber.
You ask me why?

Why, this here land's been ours for two hundred years.
Up in that graveyard they's markers
Ten generations that lived here
And died poor.

So I got to stay.
Got to keep the strip miners out
Of Grandpap's graveyard
Scratch out enough cash money
To send the youngens to school
And get 'em a little Christmas.
But don't you worry none.
When it's all over,
When the coal's give out,
The creeks is dry,
And the do-gooders have done
Give up and gone

We'll still be right here.[1]

Later, a morose and tipsy George is asked, by the visiting professor of sociology, to describe his vision of eastern Kentucky's future:

"In a hundred years," George announced profoundly, "this place where we're sitting will be in the middle of a desert. Or a garbage dump. When the coal is all gone, we may become the refuse depositary for all of the eastern United States."

"My God," laughed Amanda. "Now you've turned morbid."

"A genetic defect," said George. "I'm descended from the scum of London, you know."

"Such a pessimist," said Amanda, smiling gently. "Don't you see any hope? Any changes that could make things different?"

George shrugged. "Schools. But that won't happen until parents and taxpayers decide to value education enough to foot the bills, and that's not likely until there are jobs here for the ones who do get educated. But we can't get the industry until we improve the schools, so it's sort of a hopeless, vicious circle." He sighed. "In my home county, unemployment runs about 25 percent. Half of the ones who do work commute. A hundred to two hundred miles a day, for low-end jobs. The counties themselves are a big part of the problem. Too many, too small and poor to support good schools and services, too crooked to change."

Amanda grinned. "What about the welfare system? I assume you hate it too?"

"No," said George, "I don't. At least now nobody starves to death, or freezes, and thirty years ago that happened. I don't like the way the system penalizes the ones who want to work, but anything is better than the misery some people used to endure."

George rocked his chair back and continued. "I'll tell you what kills me. It's the hopelessness. You see so many people who've given up. They won't try any more. They've been whipped, then whipped again, and now they've quit. It all changed so fast, after World War II, that some families never did adjust. Up till then you could live pretty good without cash money. With enough kids to do the work you could scratch a living out of a hillside farm. Grow or shoot your own food, order whatever else you had to have from the Sears and Roebuck catalog, and survive if you'd work hard enough. That ain't so any more. You can work your butt off and still have to have help."

George drank more beer and stared morosely at his hands. "I'm one hell of a scholar. I preach doom, practice raising Cain. I love Eastern Kentucky but won't live here. I want it to change but I want it to stay the same. I'm full of questions, but I don't have one single damned answer."[2]

Neither, in real life, do I.

Not to the questions about eastern Kentucky's economic and political future, not to dealing with the shadowed "in-betweener's" world where some of us—natives, once removed—try to cling to both mountain ways and a more mainstream culture.

It's a strange way to live. Rooted in tradition, defensive of ways that seem peculiar to outsiders, loyal to family, friends, and community, yet—at the same time—impatient, critical, dismayed, and frustrated at the stubborn mind-set that throws up effective roadblocks to social and economic change.

My futile attempt to live in both worlds at once gets me, most often, scars, scorn, and scathing indignation from both directions. I fluctuate between a defensive angriness and a weary acceptance, having learned long ago that I can't go home again but that I really don't live in the modern new world I once wanted so badly to join.

Just how, I often ask myself, can the very same people be so painfully fragile yet so eternally resilient, so easy to hurt yet so hard to destroy?

The answer is, perhaps, very similar to how layers of earth can be so easily torn away, from topsoil to shale to sticky clay, but eventually the tearing away reaches down to the solid bare rock, which halts the erosion, stems the destruction, begins the slow process of survival and rebirth.

Some of us from the mountains, maybe most of us, are made the same way: external veneers of civilization and sophistication shatter easily—they are fragile layers of learned behavior, educated actions, and reactions—but as those layers are painfully peeled away the resistance stiffens.

The stony inner core is buried deep, sometimes carefully concealed, hidden so well that even we sometimes forget it's there.

Only when the world's pain and rejection scrape away the onionskin outer layers do we rediscover that inner rock, the inborn strength, the virtually unbreakable cornerstone of our survival.

We grew up singing about the rock of ages, the old rugged cross, amazing grace, and having to walk that lonesome valley by ourselves: those sentiments are more than mere words, more than ceremony, more than just music.

Somehow, no matter what, mountain people survive.

A people so often and so easily hurt, so frequently labeled as ignorant, ingrown, weak, defeated, and defective, who've naively trusted the corporate robbers and the cultural missionaries, somehow manage to endure.

We have the rock, the buried strength, the old values, the beliefs we turn to whenever contact with the rest of the world brings pain and failure.

Yet, during my lifetime, the reaction to my stubborn survival has been more often negative, perceived as arrogant, selfish, ignorant, or shallow, with very little understanding of the struggle against feelings of inadequacy, imperfection, unacceptability, and of being unfit.

I will not live long enough to outgrow my sense of being the awkward, backward, rejected, deficient, and out-of-place country kid. I am still eternally ill at ease with dress clothes, formal occasions, social gatherings outside the family, business meetings, and all the other necessary trappings of the life I live.

It's almost all contradiction.

From my earliest memories, so much of what was so hard for so many people was so easy for me: books, numbers, words, concepts, and the other stuff of schooling was deceptively easy but essentially frustrating, superfluous skills in a society that placed more value on physical skills, practical know-how, and the ability to fit in.

Even the faith I often speak of does not, to me, conform to conventional definitions.

I cannot totally accept the rigid doctrines of the churches of my childhood, or the social attitudes of the urban, more prosperous, and more sophisticated denominations.

I believe in animals, children, mountains, rivers, trees, seasons, and something all-powerful I cannot explain; I do not appreciate ornate buildings of worship, judgmental congregations, denominations that compete to build the grandest, own the most, carry the biggest clout, control the largest numbers of the community.

I do admire those who can so firmly believe, act out of those beliefs, who are so certain that their concepts are the right concepts.

I even envy those whose faith resolves all conflict, who turn themselves trustingly over to another's guidance.

Yet I question blind obedience to *anything*, especially the unquestioning support of doctrines that sometimes perpetuate hatred, cruelty, superiority, and harsh judgments of other humans.

I have, always, questions.

Not answers.

I wonder, often, if I should have stayed put, lived out my life close to the source. Safe, sheltered. At home.

But I know the answer. I *had* to go out and see, sample, find out for myself how life worked away from the familiar, comforting acceptance of home.

I've done that.

Not with smashing success, professional or financial, not with any shattering impact.

I've managed to survive.

Bruised and battered, prone to second guessing, weary with an effort that could have gone a more conventional direction, removed from the culture that I remember with pride but sometimes have to see in its more bleak reality.

A traveler who'd visited eastern Kentucky thirty-five years ago and now returned for a surface tour would not recognize the region. Roads, homes (mobile, palatial, and plain), motels, fast-food restaurants, new consolidated high schools, community colleges, hospitals and clinics, abandoned coal mines, flattened mountaintops, deserted downtowns, video rental stores, satellite dishes, four-wheel-drive vehicles, and discount stores are a very visible part of the progress that has filtered into the mountains.

Some things haven't changed: the illiteracy and unemployment rates still rank among the nation's highest; the politics are still colorful and crooked; basketball is still a religion; the ordinary people are still hardworking, good humored, and bonded to home and the surrounding hills.

Some changes simply are not possible. Counties will never merge; strip-mined mountains cannot be restored; coal will not last forever.

And some things should not change. The independent lifestyle, loyalty to family, pride in a rugged heritage, love for the land, deep-rooted religious faith, and a preference for the unique mountain way of living must be retained.

But stubborn pride and defensiveness can sometimes severely impede needed progress, and angry defiance of constructive criticism accomplishes nothing. We are often too proud, too hardheaded, too righteously offended to recognize the truth and act to correct our own problems.

I know firsthand the wrath of angered neighbors and relatives; I also know that I often deserve much of the backlash, that sometimes I give in to frustration and probably say some things best left unsaid. But I also firmly believe that we must look within ourselves, honestly assess our strengths and weaknesses, acknowledge that which needs changing and look for our own solutions before those solutions are handed to us by corporate landowners and a state government blinded by the "Winchester Wall." The infamous "Wall" is that mythical barrier which keeps all state effort and most tax money safely in the Bluegrass region.

I live at the very edge of that prosperous Bluegrass, but work for the institution that has served the mountains in many ways for over a century. Berea College's liberal religious and racial posture does not always sit well with much of Appalachian Kentucky (or even with the surrounding city), but Berea does not attempt to impose its values upon anyone. Berea College does teach human equality, self-examination, and service—basic virtues that every graduate carries back home or out into a broader world.

Life on a college campus does distort daily reality, does create a cushion against some harsh unpleasantness, does isolate us to some degree from the practical struggle to survive that is everyday life to many people. We are prone to talk too much, do too little, sit back and smugly tell everyone else what they ought to be doing.

As a Berea student of the early 1960s, I stubbornly resisted what I saw as efforts to homogenize me into a bland middle-class society. But, even back then, I realized that—to function with any effectiveness in the "mainstream" world—I had to learn to speak another language, slip in and out of a different culture, to learn that I could change and still retain my deep-rooted mountain ways. It's a compromise, one I'm not ashamed of, one I recommend to more eastern Kentuckians. The more we know about how the rest of the world works, the better we can pick and choose those parts of it we'd like to integrate into our own world.

I still really don't live in either the academic world or the world of my childhood; I'm still very much, as I wrote years ago for *Southern Exposure*, an "in-betweener."

Words and opinions are my only weapons. And as my fictional character said earlier, I don't have a single damned answer.

Just questions. But the very asking of those questions serves a necessary purpose, provokes needed thinking (though often at the expense of anger), and every now and then stimulates the solution to a problem.

Open discussion, complete with disagreement and even divisiveness, is the process that works. As a minor regional writer I don't speak with the clout of the late Harry Caudill; I'm not an economist, not a political scientist. One of my youthful philosophers was a Bald Hill handyman who once astutely observed that "many hands makes light work." We'd all do well to etch that old cliché firmly into our collective plans for progress.

My essays and humor won't ever save the world, certainly won't make me rich and famous, won't be quoted down through future history.

But sometimes, if I didn't write 'em, I'd just bust.

Notes

Part 1. Learning

1. "Has the Federal Money Given to the Arts Done More Harm than Good?" *Louisville Courier-Journal,* Mar. 6, 1981.
2. Moritz Bomhard, "Government 'Intervention' in the Arts Is Its Duty," *Louisville Courier-Journal,* Mar. 23, 1981.
3. "Kentucky Crafts: Traditional Quality Lies Behind Current Surge in Sales," *Louisville Courier-Journal,* Nov. 13, 1981.
4. "Mrs. Brown Took State's Crafts to the Top," *Louisville Courier-Journal,* June 19, 1983.
5. "Upgrading the Image of Appalachia," *Louisville Courier-Journal,* May 23, 1982.
6. "Council of the Southern Mountains Has Changed But Still Serves People," *Louisville Courier-Journal,* Sept. 10, 1982.
7. "A Middle View of Appalachia and 'Outsiders' Bent on Change," *Louisville Courier-Journal.* April 1, 1984.
8. "*The Dollmaker*: TV Film More Honest than Most in Showing Appalachian Life, but the Book Is Better," *Louisville Courier-Journal,* May 18, 1984.
9. Sally Bingham, "Books," *Louisville Courier-Journal,* Nov. 4, 1984.
10. "We're a Generation of 'In-betweeners,'" *Southern Exposure* 11 (3) (May–June, 1983): 172.
11. *Mitchell Tolle: American Artist* (Berea, Ky.: Painted Treasures, Inc., 1992), 51–53.
12. Wilma Dykeman and James Stokely, *The Border States* (New York: Time-Life Books, 1968), 143.
13. *Mitchell Tolle,* 87–88.
14. Ibid., 133–45.
15. Todd Pack, "Writer Says Magazine Piece Not Meant to Belittle, Brag," *Lexington Herald-Leader.* Apr. 6, 1990.
16. Faye Whitley, "Article by Elliott Native Has Upset Many Here," *Elliott County News,* undated photocopy, late Mar. or early Apr. 1990.

17. "An Open Letter to the People of Elliott Co.," *Elliott County News,* undated, late Mar. or early Apr. 1990.
18. "Home Again," *Appalachian Heritage* 18 (1) (Winter–Spring 1990): 7–10.
19. "Gone Too Long," *Appalachian Heritage* 21 (4) (Fall 1993): 26–31.
20. "Government Should Invest in Elliott County Development," *Lexington Herald-Leader,* Nov. 7, 1993.
21. "Visions of Visitors," *Kentucky Living* 48 (3) (Mar. 1994): 15–17.
22. "Artists Symbolize Elliott County's New Spirit," *Lexington Herald-Leader,* Apr. 17, 1994.
23. "Garry Barker Reflects on 'Cliffs' Project, Roots," *Elliott County News,* Dec. 31, 1993.
24. "Crafts Are Fine, but They're Not a Cure," *Lexington Herald Leader,* Mar. 11, 1990.
25. "Legislature Thinks Flea Markets, Cockfights Enough for the Mountains," *Lexington Herald-Leader,* May 9, 1990.
26. "Mountain Matriarch: For Her Family, Grandma Was a Constant among Change," *Lexington Herald-Leader,* Sept. 9, 1990.
27. "Willingness to Fight for America Being Whittled Down, Even in Patriotic Appalachia," *Lexington Herald-Leader,* Oct. 2, 1990.
28. "Video Game," *Now and Then* 8 (3) (Fall 1991): 33.
29. "Kentucky Dialect Could Give You a Certain Advantage; Bad Grammar Could Kill It," *Lexington Herald-Leader,* Sept. 15, 1991.
30. "Just Look . . . Jones Can See Real Money Woes in Elliott," *Lexington Herald-Leader,* Jan. 12, 1992.
31. Letter to the author, Jan. 20, 1992.
32. "Shame on All Those Natives of Eastern Kentucky Who Now Disdain Their Heritage," *Lexington Herald-Leader,* Mar. 1, 1992.
33. "Criticizing the Mountains Shouldn't Be Taken Personally," *Lexington Herald-Leader,* May 10, 1992.
34. "First Things First: Mountains Must Clean Up Image, Landscape," *Lexington Herald-Leader,* May 23, 1993.
35. "You Won't Hear Applause for Elliott's No. 1 Rating," *Lexington Herald-Leader,* July 11, 1993.
36. "Politics Make ARC Worthless to Eastern Kentucky," Lexington *Herald-Leader,* Aug. 15, 1993.
37. "Let's Cherish Appalachian 'Otherness,'" *Lexington Herald-Leader,* Sept. 26, 1993.

38. "Nerve Pills a Symptom of Neglect of the Region," *Lexington Herald-Leader,* Oct. 24, 1993.
39. Anonymous postcard mailed to the author, dated Oct. 26, 1993, postmarked Lexington, Kentucky.
40. "It's Not the 'Hillbilly' Image, It's the Economy," *Lexington Herald-Leader,* May 8, 1994.
41. "Targeting Aid Will Knock Kentucky out of Top 25," *Lexington Herald–Leader,* Sept. 18, 1994.

Part 2. Working

1. *Mitchell Tolle,* 44.
2. Henry D. Shapiro, *Appalachia on Our Mind: The Southern Mountains and Mountaineers in the American Consciousness, 1870–1920* (Chapel Hill: University of North Carolina Press, 1976), 242–43.
3. *The Handcraft Revival in Southern Appalachia, 1930–1990* (Knoxville: University of Tennessee Press, 1991), 167–69.
4. Frances Louisa Goodrich, *Mountain Homespun* (1931; reprint, Knoxville: University of Tennessee Press), 63.
5. "Appalachian Crafts: What Role Has the Marketplace Played in Preserving the Culture?" *The Crafts Report* 17 (June 1990): #171.
6. "The Mountain Crafts: Romancing the Marketplace," in Diversity in Appalachia: Images and Realities issue, *Journal of the Appalachian Studies Association* 5 (1993): 20–25.
7. Allen H. Eaton, *Handicrafts of the Southern Highlands* (New York: Russell Sage Foundation, 1937; reprint, New York: Dover Books, 1973), 333.
8. Jan Davidson, new introduction to *Mountain Homespun,* 1.
9. Ibid., [34].
10. Ibid., [5].
11. David Whisnant, *All That Is Native and Fine* (Chapel Hill: University of North Carolina Press, 1983), 262.
12. Eaton, *Handicrafts,* 287.
13. Ibid., 282–83.
14. Jim Wayne Miller, *The Mountains Have Come Closer* (Boone, N.C.: Appalachian Consortium Press, 1980), 40. Used with author's permission.

Part 3. Laughing

1. "Four Eyes," *Back Home in Kentucky* 11 (2) (Mar.–Apr. 1988): 41.
2. *All Night Dog* (Berea, Ky.: Kentucke Imprints, 1988), 124–27.
3. "It Ain't Easy Saying 'Dead' in One Syllable," *Salt River (Ky.) Arcadian,* Mar. 1990.
4. These columns have appeared in the *Salt River Arcadian,* the *Richmond Register,* the *Lewis County Herald,* the *Flemingsburg Gazette,* the *Berea Citizen,* and other Kentucky newspapers and journals.

Part 4. Looking

1. "The Bitter Creek Appalachian Symposium," Transformation of Life and Labor issue, *Journal of the Appalachian Studies Association* 2 (1990): 151–53.
2. Ibid., 148–49.

Bibliography

Barker, Garry. *All Night Dog.* Berea, Ky.: Kentucke Imprints, 1988.

———. "Appalachian Crafts: What Role Has the Marketplace Played in Preserving the Culture?" *The Crafts Report* 17 (June 1990): 171.

———. "The Bitter Creek Appalachian Symposium." *Transformation of Life and Labor: Journal of the Appalachian Studies Association* 2 (1990): 143–54.

———. "Four Eyes." *Back Home in Kentucky* 11 (2) (Mar.–Apr. 1988): 41.

———. "Gone Too Long." *Appalachian Heritage* 21 (4) (Fall 1993): 26–31.

———. *The Handcraft Revival in Southern Appalachia, 1930–1990.* Knoxville: University of Tennessee Press, 1991.

———. "Home Again." *Appalachian Heritage* 18 (1) (Winter–Spring 1990): 7–10.

———. *Mitchell Tolle: American Artist.* Berea, Ky.: Painted Treasures, Inc., 1992.

———. "The Mountain Crafts: Romancing the Marketplace." *Diversity in Appalachian Images and Realities. Journal of the Appalachian Studies Association* 5 (1993): 20–25.

——— "Video Game." *Now and Then* 8 (3) (Fall 1991): 33.

———. "Visions of Visitors." *Kentucky Living* 48 (3) (Mar. 1994): 15–17.

———. "We're a Generation of 'In-betweeners.'" *Southern Exposure* 11 (3) (May–June 1983): 172.

Dykeman, Wilma, and James Stokley. *The Border States.* New York: Time-Life Books, 1968.

Eaton, Allen H. *Handicrafts of the Southern Highlands.* New York: Russell Sage Foundation, 1931. Reprint, New York: Dover Books, 1973.

Elliott County News. Sandy Hook, Kentucky. 1990–94.

Goodrich, Frances Louisa. *Mountain Homespun.* 1931. Facsimile of 1931 edition with new foreword by Jan Davidson. Knoxville: University of Tennessee Press, 1989.

Lexington (Ky.) Herald-Leader. 1990–94.

Louisville (Ky.) Courier-Journal. 1981–84.

Miller, Jim Wayne. *The Mountains Have Come Closer.* Boone, N.C.: Appalachian Consortium Press, 1980.

Richmond (Ky.) Register. 1992–94.

Salt River Arcadian. Taylorsville, Ky. 1990–93.

Shapiro, Henry D. *Appalachia on Our Mind: The Southern Mountains and Mountaineers in the American Consciousness, 1870–1920.* Chapel Hill: University of North Carolina Press, 1976.

Whisnant, David. *All That Is Native and Fine: The Politics of Culture in an American Region.* Chapel Hill: University of North Carolina Press, 1983.